NOSE HILL
A Popular Guide

Beryl Hallworth *editor*

with foreword by **Mary Dover**

illustrations   **Elizabeth Allen**
                         Peter Karsten
                         Peter Allen

photographs   **Wayne Eirich**

Calgary Field Naturalists' Society
Calgary, Alberta

assistant editors	**W. Gordon Kerr**
	Wayne Eirich
design	**James B. Posey**
typesetting	**Eileen Eckert**

cover: **Prairie Crocus,** *Anemone patens*

Published by the Calgary Field Naturalists' Society, Natural Areas Group, Don Stiles, Chairman

ISBN 0-921-224-04-4

Table of Contents

Foreword
by Mary J. Dover   i

Introduction
by Beryl Hallworth 1
     Why Nose Hill Should Be Saved   1
     Location Map   2

A Geological View of Nose Hill
by Desmond Allen 3
     A Stage in the Glaciation of Southern Alberta   6
     Pre-glacial Development of the Bow Valley   10
     Glacial and Post-glacial Deposition   11

Archaeology and History of Nose Hill and Nose Creek
by Beryl Hallworth 12
     The Palaeo-Indians   12
     The Blackfoot   13
     Exploration and Settlement   16

Habitats
by Gordon Kerr 23

Introduction to Plants
by Beryl Hallworth 25
     Illustrated Glossary   25-29

Flowering Plants Other Than Grasses
by Beryl Hallworth and Gordon Kerr 30
     Flowering Periods   30
     Plants In Flower In Early Spring   30
     Plants In Flower In Spring   34
     Plants In Flower In Summer   49
     Plants In Flower In Late Summer   58

Grasses
by Linda Cole and Catharine Osborne 63
     Introduction   63
     Grasses of Nose Hill   63

Mushrooms of Nose Hill
by R.M. Danielson 70

Lichens
   by Maxwell Capen 75
     Introduction   75
     Lichens of Nose Hill   76

Mosses
   by Maxwell Capen 78
     Introduction   78
     Mosses of Nose Hill   79

Skippers and Butterflies
   by Harold Pinel 80
     Introduction   80
     Distribution   81
     Annotated List   82

Birds
   by Don Stiles 89
     How Birds are Adapted for Flight   89
     Nose Hill Birds   89

Mammals
   by Herta Przeczek 102
     Characteristics of Mammals   102
     Mammals of Nose Hill   103
     Disturbance By Man   113

Check List 114-133
     Vascular Plants   115
     Non-Vascular Plants   126
     Butterflies   128
     Birds   130
     Mammals   133

Photographs ....Plates 1-8
   by Wayne Eirich & Dave Elphinstone

Foreword

Nose Hill is an important historical site. For thousands of years the Indian tribes have camped on the hill and hunted buffalo, and there is a Palaeo-Indian site at Hawkwood that is 8000 years old. Famous explorers, such as David Thompson, Peter Fidler and botanist John Macoun, have camped on Nose Hill, and Calgary pioneers in the Nineteenth Century set up homesteads and farms in Nose Creek Valley. This publication draws attention not just to a place of local interest, but an ancient treasure, significant in the inheritance of Canada.

This Guide to Nose Hill gives us a comprehensive picture of the area, beginning with Geology, Archaeology and History. It goes on to describe the Flowering Plants, the Mushrooms, the Lichens and Mosses. These are followed by the Butterflies, Birds and Mammals. The wealth of flowers and wildlife on the Hill is truly remarkable, especially now that it is almost surrounded by houses.

I regard this book as a warning. We disregard careful preservation of these sites without considering that each is irreplaceable.

To have been invited to put my name to this Foreword, I regard as a profound compliment. The Calgary Field Naturalists' Society renders a fine service to Canada, and merits our support, and careful attention to its excellent publications.

Mary J. Dover,
C.M. (Order of Canada), O.B.E., LL.D.

Introduction

Beryl Hallworth

Why Nose Hill Should Be Saved

Nose Hill is a distinctive feature — it rises 90 metres above the city of Calgary, and forms a splendid background. It is part of the landscape that we take for granted — it has always been there, always an outstanding feature. It has an unbroken skyline which implies open country beyond. West of Nose Hill Park the lovely lines of the hill have already been blotted out by rows of houses. Can you imagine what a disaster it would be if Nose Hill Park got blotted out the same way? It would not only cause a storm of protest, but it would be too late to do anything about it — Nose Hill would be lost to us.

There is a wide variety of wildlife on the hill. The 1987 check-list, made by the Calgary Field Naturalists, gives an impressive total for the area: 91 bird species have been reported, also many butterflies and moths. Although 17 mammals have been seen on the hill, many of these are now rarely seen, because of the disturbance caused by the nearby housing sub-divisions. Flowers continue to flourish, however, with over 200 species being recorded. In spring, summer and fall they are a continual delight. Nose Hill is Calgary's largest area of relatively undisturbed prairie. Where else in the city could you take a visitor interested in prairie grasses?

There are many interesting archaeological remains on Nose Hill — an Indian camp kill-site, many tipi rings and hearths, and buffalo rubbing stones, to name only a few. The area was popular with the Blackfoot and Peigan tribes because the strong winds blew off the snow cover in winter, exposing the grass, on which the buffalo could feed. So much of the Indian heritage in Alberta has already been destroyed — it would be criminal to destroy any more.

A big city like Calgary needs parks. We are surrounded by houses, roads, gas fumes and hordes of people. We badly need some wide open spaces, and a "wide open space" aptly describes Nose Hill, a hill for all seasons.

Location

The area referred to as "Nose Hill" in this book is bounded on the south by John Laurie Boulevard, on the east by 14 Street N.W., on the west by Shaganappi Trail, and on the north by MacEwan Glen residential sub-division. The area is contained within Section 32, Township 24, Range 1, west of the Fifth Meridian; and Sections 4, 5, 6, 7, 8 and 9, Township 25, Range 1, west of the Fifth Meridian.

There is a map of Nose Hill at the back of the book.

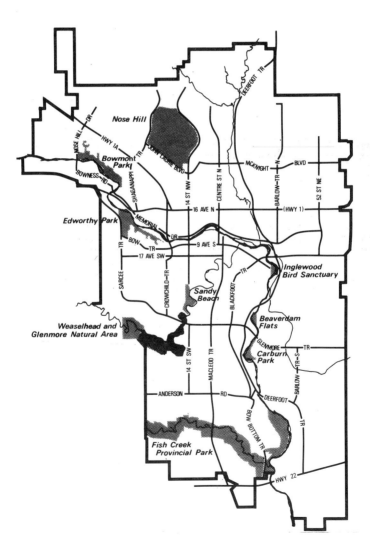

A Geological View of Nose Hill
Desmond Allen

Choose a clear, warm morning and climb to the rock outcrops on the hillside north-east of the junction of Charleswood Drive and John Laurie Boulevard. This is a good point from which to reconstruct the geological events which shaped Nose Hill and the beautiful scenery stretching away to the southern and western horizons.

The rock outcrop you have reached is an example of the bedrock of the Calgary area. If you dug deeply enough anywhere in Calgary you would eventually find the same or similar rock. In many parts of Calgary it is quite deeply buried under soft surface silts or gravels. In other places, such as on many hillsides, it is close to the surface, and may outcrop. You would also find the same rocks below the surface in a wide region around Calgary. You would find them at Cochrane and south through Priddis and in the Porcupine Hills. In fact, these rocks are known as the Porcupine Hills Formation by most geologists. The rocks are composed of shale beds alternating with sandstone beds, but the sandstone predominates.

The outcrop you are looking at is composed of thin curved sheets of greenish-grey sand which was probably laid down as a sand-bar in a river bed. This type of curved bedding is often called current-bedding by geologists. Current-bedded sandstone is frequently seen in the Porcupine Hills Formation, but it is often replaced by much thicker beds of sandstone, which makes a beautiful, if rather soft, building stone. Many of Calgary's older buildings were made of this stone.

When the Porcupine Hills Formation was being laid down some 60 million years ago, the Calgary area had quite different scenery — somewhat dull compared with the hills and mountains of today. In those times the area was close to sea level. A bird a thousand feet above the land which is now Nose Hill would have seen a flat landscape covered by deciduous forest, swamps, and broad, slow rivers. North, south, east and west this great flat wilderness stretched monotonously to the horizon. To the east, the bird might have seen inlets or bays of a sea or lakes. There were no shining Rockies to the west. Slow meandering rivers came out of mountainous regions, away beyond the western horizon, in what is now central B.C., and dropped their sediments in the lowlands to form our bed-rock.

Sandstones are seldom found to be very fossiliferous and our outcrop has no fossils in it. Elsewhere in the city, beautiful deciduous leaf-remains have been found in the sandstones, and well-preserved fresh-water clam shells in the shales. Our ancient bird's landscape was probably teeming with life in a relatively warm, humid climate. The dinosaurs had already died out and been replaced by a predominance of fairly recognizable mammals and birds. Man was still far in the future.

When you stand right on top of Nose Hill, you will notice that the top is quite flat, and you will also notice that the top of Broadcast Hill (the hill on the other side of the Bow Valley, where the Olympic ski-jumps have been built) is also flat and at about the same level. The same level is repeated in the tops of the hills around Priddis, away to the south. The Nose, Broadcast, and Priddis Hill tops may be remnants of the old swampy, forested surface only slightly modified by later geological events.

What happened to change our part of Alberta from a steamy, swampy, low-lying wooded area to a high, dry, windy grassland? Enormous compressive forces within the crust of the earth had been building up slowly along the western borders of our area. Eventually, great north-south fractures split the crust and the forces were relieved by plates of crust moving over and under one another to form a great mountain chain 60 miles to the west. At the same time the old flat land previously close to sea level was lifted up towards its present elevation. The great upheavals probably happened gradually over many millions of years. Certainly, there would have been frequent, violent earthquakes, but the mountain chain which stretches from Alaska through the Canadian Rockies, through the United States, through Central America and the Andes of South America probably rose up slowly. This great change in elevation of our area was accompanied by vast changes in climate and drainage. The new rivers flowing out of the high, young mountains were fast and carried vast quantities of sand and pebbles. A slight lessening of the stream speed would result in accumulation of gravel until the stream channel became blocked, and the stream had to move sideways to a new course. In those early days of the new landscape the rivers had not sorted themselves out into definite valleys. They laid down beds of gravel over wide areas of the early elevated plains where thick sheets of river gravels were deposited. These gravels have already been exploited by surface excavation as can be seen at the top of the hill to the west of 14 Street.

Eventually, the drainage from the new mountains became confined into definite courses and the long process of erosion, which resulted in the beautiful Bow and Elbow valleys, began. However, the story of Calgary's geology and landscape was far from over, and perhaps the most spectacular events were still to come.

About two million years ago, the climate started to get much colder in the northern hemisphere. At that time the rivers had cut our Calgary landscape to more or less its present shape. With the general lowering of temperature, snow falling in the mountains and on the north-facing slopes of valleys no longer completely melted in the shorter summers. Year after year the colder weather persisted, and the glaciers in the mountains started to advance down to the valleys and out towards the east. In North-Central Canada, the snows were particularly heavy and little summer melting took place. There, the weight of snow soon converted the older snow below into ice, and in time thick glaciers were formed. The map shows how the glaciers from North-Central Canada (the Laurentide Ice Sheet) moved out to the south-east, south and south-west. Eventually, the south-western moving ice met the glaciers (the Cordilleran Ice Sheet) extending as tongues out of the Rocky Mountain valleys. The great ice sheets from North-Central Canada were of much greater strength than the tongues from the mountains, and as a result, mountain glaciers were deflected to the south. As can be seen on the map, the tongues from the mountains around Jasper would have been squeezed into a south-moving stream between the great Central Canadian sheet and the tongues emerging from the mountains further south.

The Jasper stream rode right across Nose Hill. It is a particularly interesting ice-stream because when it passed through the mountains near Jasper great blocks of a very distinctive quartzite fell from the peaks onto the glacier surface, or were plucked by the glacier from the valley sides. This rock had been laid down as a coarse sandstone in the distant Cambrian time, some 500 million years ago. It is an extremely hard and durable rock in which the original grains of sand or grit have been fused together into a cohesive mass. The Jasper rock was so strong that even the great forces in the glaciers did not break it up, and today we find large blocks of it in a fairly narrow band stretching southwards over Nose Hill, through Okotoks to Northern Montana. The "Great Rock" southwest of Okotoks is the largest example, but there are thousands of smaller ones to be seen, some of them on Nose Hill. They were greatly prized as scratching posts by buffalo in later years, and are often found to be highly polished by the rubbing of countless animals. A good example occurs on the east side of the hill above 14 Street, near the 64 Avenue N.W. entrance to Nose Hill. Another fine example known as "Split Rock" lies in the bottom of the valley of Nose Creek, just east of Simons Valley Drive.

In fact, each glacier carried with it blocks of the rocks over which it had passed and, eventually, when the ice melted, these were dropped as erratics on the surface of the land. We can trace the course of the various ice streams by the erratics lying on the surface today. East of Calgary we would expect to find boulders of granite and other

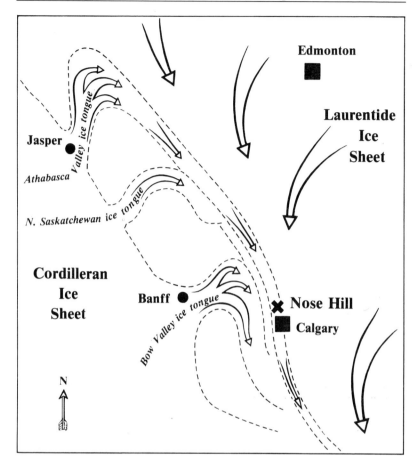

Tongues of ice from the Cordilleran Ice Sheet flowed eastwards out of
the mountains and were deflected southwards by the large Laurentide
Ice Sheet.

A Stage in the Glaciation
of Southern Alberta

crystalline rocks from North-Central Canada and, in fact, if we walk across ploughed fields to the east of the Airport, we will find such boulders. In some places the boulders are so common that the farmers had to collect them into piles before tilling the land. On Nose Hill we find boulders of Cambrian quartzite from near Jasper and other material from the mountains. Blocks of local bedrock, sandstone, were also picked up by the moving ice and dropped when the ice melted. To the west we find boulders which can be matched to the rocks forming the mountains near Banff. But the kings among erratics were those from near Jasper. Most other erratics of our area are quite small in comparison.

Imagine for a moment the scene at the height of the Ice Age. Our hills and valleys would have been buried under great thicknesses of slowly-moving ice. During the long winters the only relief from white would have been the few frost-grimed erratics carried on the surface of the glaciers and the occasional peak showing through, where the mountain ice bulged down from the Rockies. It is unlikely that any form of life could have been seen. During the short summers the scene would have been transformed. The surface of the ice sheet would have had its own summer drainage system with the incredible blue-green of the ice below showing through the clear water of the multitudes of melt-streams and small lakes. Perhaps the occasional water bird blown off its migration route would have rested on the blue lakes. Rest would have been the only reason for stopping. There would have been little, if any, food in the lakes. In those places where the ice tongues were forced into new directions, for example, where the mountain ice tongues were deflected southwards by the stronger mass of ice, cracks or crevasses would have developed in the ice and the streams would have cascaded into these to flow away in caves through and under the ice.

At least two temporary retreats of the ice took place in North America and during these retreats the glaciers disappeared and relatively warm climate conditions prevailed. The last improvement in climate started only 15,000 years ago and since then the ice has retreated steadily. No one knows for sure, but many believe that we are in just another interglacial warm spell and that in the future the weather will deteriorate once more and that the ice will come again.

When the climate improved in Southern Alberta, some 15,000 years ago, the mountain glaciers no longer increased in weight each year and the amount of ice melted exceeded the amount accumulated. The net result was the retreat of the mountain ice. The stronger ice sheets from North Central Canada were probably more persistent, perhaps because they were thicker in the first place, or perhaps because the climate did not improve as fast in the regions of their source.

The waters cascading from the ice surface probably melted the ice quickly around the crevasses under these improved climatic conditions. The Calgary area was at one of the hinge points, where the Bow Valley ice had been deflected southwards and many crevasses had probably formed. It is likely that the ice melted away from these hinge points first. Once the melting had begun, more and more land showed from beneath the ice each summer and this land would have been littered with untidy mounds of mixed silt, sand, gravel and boulders dropped during the melting processes. These unsorted mounds of glacial material (known as glacial till) may be seen very well if you drive north from Crowchild Trail along 85 Street N.W. They form beautiful small hills and hollows at the west end of Nose Hill.

At first the melt-waters would have flowed away in a drainage pattern under the glaciers to the east and south, but these drainage patterns were incapable of handling the vast quantities of water and sediment to come. Eventually, they became blocked and the melt-waters collected in a lake, which we call Glacial Lake Calgary. This lake stretched from the base of Nose Hill over the present downtown area, away towards the south and up the Bow Valley towards Cochrane.

When Glacial Lake Calgary existed, the summer scene from the top of Nose Hill can be imagined. To the east, the great Northern ice stands as white and green cliffs above the turquoise of the lake. Occasionally, masses of ice break off and drop with enormous splashes to float away down wind as icebergs. Hills stand up out of the lake as islands. Broadcast Hill stands high with quite a low ridge running eastwards from there through what is now Strathcona and Mount Royal. The land is almost devoid of life. Perhaps, the odd tuft of grass or small alpine plant has managed to establish itself. Perhaps, a few birds stop for a short rest on their migrations to and from more hospitable places. The lake is quite blue, except where the many streams carry plumes of brown silt out from the brown land. In places, remnants of the glaciers cap the hills and fill the side valleys. Away to the west, tongues of ice can still be seen where they extend out from the mountain valleys or down from the peaks and ridges.

Glacial Lake Calgary has left a legacy to Calgary in the form of thick fine sediments lying on top of the mounds of glacial till beneath. Those fine sediments are mostly composed of powdered limestone, "rock flour", from the mountains. The old lake bottom is easily picked out. It forms the relatively flat area running out from the base of Nose Hill a few hundred yards south of John Laurie Boulevard. On it, we built the University, Southern Alberta Institute of Technology, McMahon Stadium, Market Mall, the Jubilee Auditorium, and many homes. From your vantage point on Nose Hill you can pick out the flat bottom of the lake in many different areas. Gardeners in these areas sometimes regret the extremely good drainage caused by up to 100 feet of the fine glacial lake deposits. They may also notice that the soil in their gardens is extremely limey.

Life probably came back to the cold desert quite quickly. Migrating birds which had fed on seeds in other areas dropped them randomly and some seeds found conditions suitable for germination. Many wind-blown seeds also took root. The resulting grasslands were soon alive with many species of insect, and nesting birds were not long in taking advantage of the insect and seed food provided. The conditions were excellent for grazing animals and great herds could have been seen on the treeless prairie which advanced northwards close on the heels of the retreating ice. Man had arrived in North America (from Siberia, over the Bering land-bridge) towards the end of the last glaciation and had occupied the warm areas towards the south of the continent. The tribes soon moved north to exploit the great herds of bison and other hoofed animals.

Since Glacial Lake Calgary drained away, perhaps 10,000 years ago, the Bow River has cut down through the soft fine lake sediments, through the mounds of glacial till beneath, and into the bedrock. The lake sediments can be seen as vertical cliffs on the north side of the Bow River across from Bowness, and in Scotsmans Hill across the Elbow River from the Stampede Grounds. The bottoms of the river valleys are filled with gravel bars laid down recently. The excavations for buildings in the downtown area have to contend with this river gravel deposit.

The diagrams will help to summarize the geology of the Calgary area. They are greatly simplified geological cross-sections from Nose Hill to Broadcast Hill. Various stages of the development of the Bow Valley are shown. Also shown are the sediments accumulated at these various stages starting with the early river-gravels on top of Nose Hill followed by hummocks of poorly sorted glacial till which in the valley were later buried under the fine-grained material which collected at the bottom of Glacial Lake Calgary. The final stage shows how the Bow River has cut through the glacial deposits and is now forming its own gravel base along its new bed.

Further Reading

Jackson, L.E., M.C. Wilson (Eds.) 1987 *Geology of the Calgary Area.* Canadian Society of Petroleum Geologists
Hardy, W.G. (Ed.) 1967 *Alberta: A Natural History.* Hurtig Publishers, Edmonton, Alberta

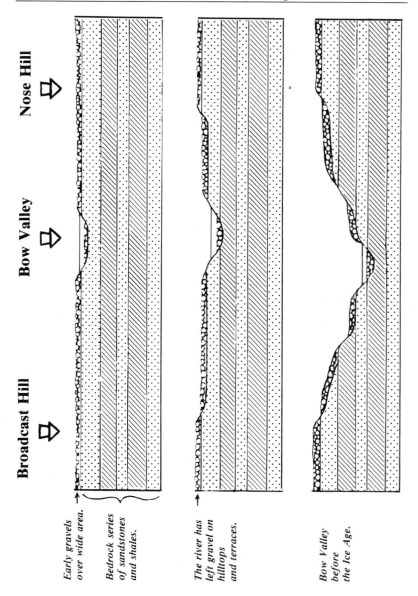

Nose Hill ⇨

Bow Valley ⇨

Broadcast Hill ⇨

Early gravels over wide area.

Bedrock series of sandstones and shales.

The river has left gravel on hilltops and terraces.

Bow Valley before the Ice Age.

Pre-glacial Development of the Bow Valley

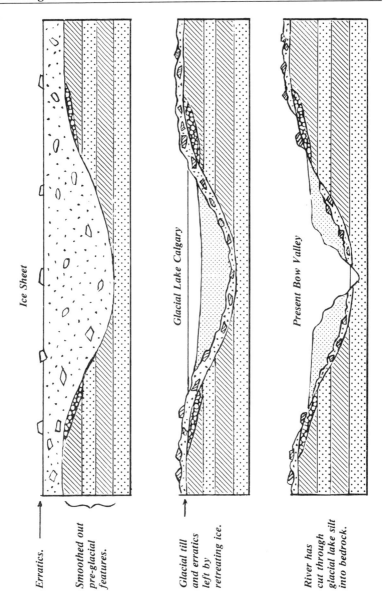

Ice Sheet

Erratics.

Smoothed out pre-glacial features.

Glacial Lake Calgary

Glacial till and erratics left by retreating ice.

Present Bow Valley

River has cut through glacial lake silt into bedrock.

Glacial and Post-glacial Deposition

Archaeology and History of
Nose Hill and Nose Creek Beryl Hallworth

The Palaeo-Indians

There is a very interesting Palaeo-Indian campsite, about 8000 years old, just west of Nose Hill, at Hawkwood, now a residential subdivision of the City of Calgary. The Nose Hill Uplands extend from a point opposite downtown Calgary to Cochrane, and Hawkwood is on the South-West escarpment. This was a favourable site for humans and buffalo, because these South-Western slopes are often blown clear of snow in winter, exposing the grass; also, the frequent Chinooks result in a less chilly environment.

Six levels of occupation have been found at the campsite — the lowest one is approximately 8250 years old, far older than the Pyramids of Egypt. The next 2 levels above it belong to the Early Mummy Cave period, about 6800 years old. This period takes its unusual name from a cave found east of Yellowstone National Park. These 2 levels are below a band of Mazama Ash. This volcanic ash was carried north by the winds from a huge eruption of Mount Mazama, in Oregon, 6500 years ago. This eruption resulted in the formation of the well-known Crater Lake. This layer of ash, which is similar to the ash from the recent and much smaller eruption of Mount St. Helens, is very useful to archaeologists, because it can be definitely dated.

There are 3 levels above the Mazama Ash deposit; level 4 is dated to the Mummy Cave period, and level 5 belongs to the Oxbow period, 4600 -3000 years ago. The top level (6) is of late Prehistoric Age, 1750 - 230 years ago.

There were nearly 300 artifacts found at this site, including stone scrapers, choppers, and many projectile points ("arrow-heads") for spears, darts, and atlatls. The atlatls were called "spear-throwers"; they were clever wooden devices that were designed to give spears more force and range. These spears had small projectile points.

Some of the stone tools found at this site must have been traded; an Avon Chert tool was found from Avon, near Helena, Montana; also a tool made from Etherington Chert, from the Livingstone Range in

Kananaskis Country. There was, also, a tool made of Beaver Creek Quartzite — this rock is very rare in the Calgary area, but is found in North-Eastern Alberta. These examples show that trade was carried on between the various Indian tribes.

The Hawkwood camp was used by the Palaeo-Indians as a light butchering site; the bones found were mostly limb bones, the heavy butchery of the carcases must have been done nearby. The animal bones were mostly Buffalo, but bones of Deer, Elk, Moose, Dog, Fox and Rabbit were also found. The site was also used for tool-making and for the manufacture of hides.

The Hawkwood site was developed by Melcor Development Ltd., and they commissioned Lifeways of Canada Ltd. to do an Archaeological Survey before any building took place. Dr. Brian Reeves was the Scientific Advisor.

The Blackfoot

The area around Nose Hill was later dominated by the Blackfoot, who entered the area in the 1700's. There were three tribes in the Blackfoot Nation, the Blackfoot proper, the Bloods and the Peigans. These were Plains Indians. There were frequent skirmishes with their traditional enemies, the Crees. The Peigans were more war-like than the Blackfoot and the Bloods, and were found further west. There is plenty of evidence that the Peigans camped on Nose Hill, and in Nose Creek. They hunted the buffalo; their whole economy revolved around the buffalo herds. Nose Hill was so exposed that the winds blew the snow away in the winter, exposing the grass on which the buffalo fed. The Stoney Indians, who lived in the foothills, also came into the plains to hunt buffalo.

Some interesting features on Nose Hill are the buffalo rubbing-stones. When the animals were molting, the loose hairs were irritating, and the buffalo walked round and round the stones, rubbing the hairs off, and formed deep depressions around the stones. Sometimes these were rubbed smooth. These large boulders are "erratics" from the Mount Edith Cavell area in Jasper National Park, carried down by the glaciers of the Pleistocene Age. They are found strewn all the way from the Park across the foothills and the prairie to Okotoks, where the "Big Rock" is a distinctive feature. This line of erratics continues into Montana and is called the Foothills Erratic Train. The "Split Rock" in Nose Creek is another example. It was revered by the Indians and was also used as a buffalo rubbing-stone.

There are many tipi-rings on Nose Hill, showing that the Plains Indians frequently camped there. The stones forming the rings were placed there to hold down the buffalo hides forming the tipis. Sometimes the hearth stones can be seen in the centre of the circle. Robert Aramant, a former member of the Natural Areas group of The Calgary Field Naturalists' Society, made a detailed study of these rings, and in 1983 produced a comprehensive account of them, with numerous maps of the 6 areas he had studied on Nose Hill. He described 60 tipi-rings.

McPherson Creek is a tributary of Nose Creek, and McPherson Coulee is especially rich in Indian heritage. Indian pictographs are rare in the Calgary area, but several are found in the coulee and are illustrated in the Rev. Stephen Wilk's book, "One Day's Journey". They were called the "Picture Rocks", and the coulee was called "Writing Coulee".

The cliffs of the coulee were used as a buffalo jump, where herds of buffalo were driven over, and then killed. A vast number of buffalo can be killed in this way. We have a graphic description by Bert Clayton, a pioneer settler, in 1900: "The buffalo bones were nine feet deep, and covered an acre." These bones were collected by the early settlers and taken in carts to the nearest railway station, then sent to Eastern Canada to be made into glue. The settlers made quite an amount of money this way. The bones piled up in great heaps at the railway stations. Regina's name was "Pile of Bones" until it was made the capital of Saskatchewan, when the City Council decided "Regina" was more dignified!

In 1867, Addison McPherson established a trading post in the coulee, and it was called Fort McPherson. It was said that he was a Hudson Bay Company trader. Mr. E.M. Clayton, a pioneer settler, describes him as "a fearless, adventurous youth, who hunted and trapped with the Indians." Whiskey Creek flows into the McPherson Creek, and on the banks is a large cave where a whiskey still is said to have been operated.

The material used for the stone tool workshops came from the quartzite cobbles that outcrop on the surface of the hill. These cobbles would not be found elsewhere in the North Calgary area, except along river-banks, because the land is covered by thick silt deposits from Glacial Lake Calgary. These deposits are shown in the diagrams illustrating the previous chapter on the Geology of the hill.

The following quotation from the Reeves report reminds us that these Indian sites should be carefully preserved: "While a particular type of site, a tipi-ring for example, is still relatively common today, each represents a unique event, which, once gone, cannot be replaced."

When the fur traders came with blankets and guns to exchange them for the furs brought by the Indians, they also brought beads and mirrors. The mirrors were popular with the women, and with the men, because they used them for signalling. Spy Hill, a westward continuation of Nose Hill, has a small "peak", altitude 4200 feet. This was often used for signalling, hence the name "Spy Hill".

There was an interesting article in the Calgary Herald on March 13, 1897, which is quoted below:

"A day or two ago, the body of an Indian was found in Nose Creek, enclosed in a box. Word was brought into town and the Indian being said to be a Blackfoot, Major McGibbon wired to Mr. M. Begg, informing him of the fact. Mr. Begg, accompanied by Dr. Porter (coroner), and Dr. McDood, visited the scene. Major Jarvis provided the transport, with a number of policemen. An Indian prisoner was also taken to the spot to assist in identification of the remains.

"The doctor found the Indian to have been a young man about 30 years old, who had died from natural causes. The Indian prisoner identified the body as that of Running Weasel, who died across the Bow last fall, the remains being placed in the position in which they were found, by the well-known Indian, Deerfoot, at the request of the deceased, when dying. He, it is reported, to have asked 'to be put where he could see the great city grow beneath his feet.' He was buried by the police interpreter yesterday."

Mr. James Rogers, a graduate student in the Department of Archaeology at the University of Alberta, Calgary (before the university was autonomous in 1966), studied the Indian sites on Nose Hill. He found a camp kill-site, north of 73 Street N.W. near a spring. Near the Huntington Hills community he found 8 large tipi rings, averaging 15 feet in diameter. In a ravine one mile west of 4th Street N.W. he found 5 large tipi rings, and nearby were large quantities of fire-broken rock.

Dr. Brian Reeves, in 1978, made an Historical Resources Inventory and assessment of Nose Hill Park and found forty-two prehistoric sites. These include seven tipi ring sites, a stone cairn/effigy, three stone tool workshops, and fourteen scatters of stone artifacts. A possible Bison kill was found in a coulee.

The name "Nose Hill" probably came from the Blackfoot. "When a society of braves, who policed the women, found one unfaithful to the tribe, they cut off her nose as an example to the rest." This information came from two members of the Blackfoot tribe; one was a woman, Many Owls (Mrs. Bad Old Man), who was 90 years old in 1942, and the other was Stump (Big Eagle), who was 70 years old at the time. This explanation of the name "Nose Hill" came from Frances Fraser, who studied Indian folk-lore and customs. The nose-cutting practice continued until the 1890's, when it was forbidden. One victim of this barbarous custom was the wife of the Indian, Skunk, and she lived until the 1900's. This explanation seems the most probable one. There is a second theory, which gives a possible explanation of the name. It was suggested by a pioneer woman, Mrs. Pat Clayton, and supported by other pioneers. She said there was a legend that a long time ago, a party of Indians camped by the spring in Nose Creek and obtained some "firewater". They became drunk and quarrelsome, and in the fight that followed, one of the women had her nose bitten off — hence "Nose Creek", and the nearby hill was "Nose Hill".

Exploration and Settlement

There were several famous people associated with the area. David Thompson, the well-known explorer and map-maker, spent the winter of 1787/1788 with the Peigan Indians in the Bow Valley. As the tribe frequented Nose Hill, it is very likely that he accompanied them when they hunted the buffalo there. He left the Hudson Bay Company, and joined the North-Westers. In 1800 he returned to the Bow Valley with Duncan McGillivray, a well-known fur-trader. Thompson records a visit to the Nose Hill area in his Journal for November 2nd, 1800.

Peter Fidler was a fur trader who had joined the Hudson Bay Company and spent the winter of 1789/1790 at Cumberland House with David Thompson. During that winter, they were both taught surveying by Philip Turnor, the official Surveyor for the Company. Fidler records in his Journal that he was in the Nose Hill area in December 1792. He describes a trip with the Peigan Indians on December 7th, and saw Nose Creek and the range of hills beyond. He describes them as follows, "These hills run in a parallel direction with the Rocky Mountains from their northern termination near Devil's Head (near Lake Minnewanka) and their south end terminates at the banks of this river (the Bow). They are high and run in four parallels with the mountains." He also recorded the temperature on the day as 58 °F, which is rather high for December, but Alberta weather is notoriously fickle.

The Palliser Expedition, led by John Palliser and James Hector, passed this area in the summer of 1858. They camped near present-day Innisfail and shot 17 Buffalo. They called their camp "Slaughter Camp". Then they moved south to the Bow Valley, probably along Nose Creek Valley.

Another interesting character associated with the area was the Methodist preacher, George McDougall. He came west in 1860 and built a church in Victoria (now called Pakan), which was 90 miles Northeast of Edmonton. His son, John McDougall, travelled to the Morleyville area (present-day Morley) in 1875, and began building a church there, the first church in the area. This church can still be seen, close to the 1A Highway. His father joined him in the winter of 1875 to help him. The food supply was running low, and on January 18, 1876, father and son set off together on a buffalo hunt. They camped somewhere near Nose Creek. By January 24, they had shot six buffalo, and set off back to their camp. Just before they reached camp, George McDougall rode on ahead in the darkness. He said he would cook the supper, but he never reached the camp. John organized a search party, but they could not find him that night. The next day some hunters reported seeing a man on horseback who appeared unwell, or disoriented, riding in circles. Then a severe snow storm occurred and the search was held up. It was not until February 6 that McDougall's frozen body was found on the east side of Nose Creek, about 12 miles from their camp. A memorial cairn has been erected on the spot where his body was found. It was unveiled on September 16, 1960, by the Historical Society of Alberta, Calgary chapter. This date was chosen because it was 100 years after George McDougall was appointed as a missionary to Western Canada. When last seen the cairn was riddled with bullet holes, a shocking case of vandalism.

John Macoun, "the Father of Canadian Botany", was another famous visitor to Nose Hill. He was an Irishman, who had emigrated to Canada with his family in 1850, and became a very well-known naturalist. In 1879, he was asked by the Canadian Government to lead a field trip to the prairies to study Natural History. He eventually arrived at Fort Calgary (built 4 years before), and records in his Autobiography, "We camped under Nose Hill where there was a Fort, and visited the Fort... At this time there was only one house at the site of the present Calgary and that was the I.J. Baker's Store [I.G. Baker] and the clerk from whom I bought a few necessaries, was Mr. King, now Postmaster of Calgary." At that time, Calgary was still a tent city — the Canadian Pacific Railway did not come through until 1883.

A less-well-known figure, but nonetheless important to the Canadian West, was Colonel Robertson-Ross, the Adjutant-General of the Canadian Militia. He was sent by the Government to make a reconnaissance of Western Canada in 1872. He left Fort Garry (Winnipeg), and eventually arrived at Rocky Mountain House in September, 1872. He and his party rode south to McPherson Coulee and camped there, and then rode south to the area of present-day Calgary (Fort Calgary was not built until three years later). On their travels, the party had seen three wolves and numerous antelope. The Alberta Historical Review, Summer Edition, 1961, displays a map showing the route taken by Colonel Robertson-Ross. It followed the Rocky Mountain Traders' Trail, which came south along the west of Nose Creek Valley and past the Nose Creek Spring. This is probably the route followed by David Thompson. It took the Robertson-Ross party 5½ hours from McPherson's Coulee to Nose Hill Spring. On November 4, 1974 the Nose Creek Historical Society and the R.C.M.P. Centennial Committee unveiled a plaque in his memory. On his return to Ottawa he advised the Government to send a mounted militia to control the West, as it was badly needed. They took his advice, and acted with remarkable speed. In 1873, the North West Mounted Police detachment was set up, and in 1874 they began the "Long March West" to build Fort Macleod.

Wolves were still found in the Nose Hill area in the 1890's and they destroyed pioneers' calves. One large wolf lived near Split Rock in the West Nose Creek Valley, and when Joe Lewis was returning to his shack early one night, with a team of horses, the wolf followed him. When he reached his shack he fetched a gun and shot the wolf. Afterwards, "the wolf's head, hide and all" were proudly displayed in the front room of his shack.

Coyotes were hunted on horseback with a pack of hounds in Nose Creek Valley in the early 1900's, and there were a number of bobcats in the area in the 1920's. Beaver dams were found in the West Nose Creek; even as late as the 1970's there were at least fifteen dams there. A Lynx was twice reported in the Nose Hill area in 1973/1974. H. Hanson shot a 300 lb. bear in 1949.

In this Automobile Age, it is very difficult for us to realize that around the turn of the century, life revolved around horses. If you wanted to go anywhere, you either travelled on horseback, or in a buggy, or a democrat, or by stagecoach. Some travelled in a horse-omnibus. All farm work was done by horses and oxen; all the operations, such as ploughing and threshing, involved horses. All these hundreds of horses needed hay and oats. These were supplied by the farms north of Calgary; the native prairie hay was called "prairie wool" *(Bouteloua gracilis)*. The hay was brought into Calgary along the "Hay Trails" which wound their way across the prairie, and they all ended at the Haymarket, which was just opposite the old Langevin Bridge. One of these Hay Trails came down from the north, passing Nose Hill on the West, and joined the old "McDougall Trail" from Morley to Calgary. Another came down West Nose Creek Valley along the eastern edge of Nose Hill. To quote C. Redvers Perry, "The Hay Trail was Calgary's first energy pipeline, and also served for a well-worn path for the settlers and their families to go to town and shop for their weekly provisions."

The pioneer work done by the surveyors is often overlooked; they ventured into unknown territories, fording creeks and rivers, coping with marshes, muskegs, mosquitoes, and many other problems. A survey party consisted of eight men, accompanied by pack horses, or a covered wagon, with 66-foot chains. Although a few settlers had drifted into the area around Nose Hill, no real settlement could take place until the district had been surveyed. In June 1880, Montague Aldous, DLS, DTS, surveyed the 5th Meridian, which is 114 degrees West from the Greenwich Meridian in London. He surveyed the Meridian from Stoney Plain, near Edmonton, to the United States border. This is one of the three control Meridians for the township system of land settlement in Alberta. Once the line had been established, ranges and townships could be plotted and settlement could proceed. (No. 2 highway from Calgary to Edmonton runs more or less along the 5th Meridian.) By 1883, 27,000,000 acres had been surveyed and 1221 townships had been created. In 1884, Samual Brabason, another surveyor, was sent to the Nose Hill area and wrote about Township 25, Range 1, "this township is all open prairie heavily rolling and hilly, particularly in the southwest portion where Nose Hill attains considerable altitude above the Bow River....an abundant supply of excellent water may be had from the Nose Creek, a beautiful clear stream about 4 feet wide and 2½ deep with gravelly bottom."

The Canadian Pacific Railway reached Calgary in 1883, and this naturally resulted in a surge of immigrants eager to settle in or near the town. Some of this settlement spilled over into the West Nose Creek Valley, which was later called Symon's Valley, after Symon, a farmer, who became Postmaster in the early 1900's. There is a bronze plaque to honour the pioneer surveyors at the site of Dickson-Stevenson Stopping Place on the old Edmonton Trail, sponsored by the Nose Creek Historical Society.

After a disastrous fire in Calgary in 1886, when many of the wooden buildings were destroyed, the houses were rebuilt with sandstone; in fact, Calgary was known as the "Sandstone City". Vast quantities of this building material were brought in from the sandstone quarries around the city. Some of this came from the quarries on the north-east side of West Nose Creek. A date, 1891, is carved above one of these quarries. The stone was cut at the site and carried to Calgary on carts drawn by horses. Sandstone from the J.A. Lewis quarry was used for the entrance to the Imperial Bank and part of the "new" City Hall (1909). Stone from Nose Creek quarries was used for building James Short School and the old Court House. By 1915 sandstone was no longer in demand; it was replaced by limestone and brick. Hay's quarry at Beddington, near Split Rock, did very little business in 1915. Sandstone cut and shaped at the quarry cost $20 a cord (128 cubic feet). The sandstone escarpment is one of the striking features of Symon's Valley, and this "Paskapoo" sandstone outcrops on the south, facing the slope of Nose Hill. The correct name for this sandstone layer is the Porcupine Hills Formation.

As a tribute to the stone cutters, quarry-men, and labourers of the sandstone quarries, the Nose Creek Historical Society has preserved and restored a Sandstone Quarry Winch which was originally imported from Welland, Ontario, in the 1880's. It was worked by horse-power and was last used in 1912. It had lain neglected in Symon's Valley until 1968, when the Society decided to restore it. After a great deal of work, it was fully restored, put into working order, and in 1980 it was placed at the entrance to the Calgary Co-op Shopping Centre in Beddington Heights.

There were nine springs in West Nose Creek Valley (Symon's Valley), and one of these is the Nose Hill Spring. It lies at the South end of the valley, near the place where West Nose Creek joins the main Nose Creek. These springs were focal points for the settlers, who all needed a good supply of fresh water. The Nose Hill Spring had a constant flow of water and was well-known. On Wednesday, June 25, 1898, it was the setting for a mid-summer entertainment, with "refreshments galore", and a Sports Day followed. Among the guests present was George Murdoch, Calgary's first Mayor. Part of the land around the spring was owned by Patrick Burns, the wealthy owner of the meat-packing firm. There were many cattle and horses rounded up here, and there were several "branding bees."

In July, 1966, at a meeting of the Nose Creek Farmer's Union, C. Redvers Perry suggested that a cairn should be set up at the site of the spring to commemorate the pioneer farmers, settlers and cattlemen of the West Nose Creek Valley. The suggestion met with unanimous approval. The owners of the land, Carma Developers, co-operated with the project and improved the site, with the help of the Nose Creek Farmers Union. The cairn was officially unveiled in October 1968 by Jack Leslie, Mayor of Calgary.

At one time, the southern part of Nose Creek, north of St. George's Island, had a somewhat unsavoury reputation, because it was one of the best-known of Calgary's "Red Light" districts, and there were some colourful characters associated with it, Diamond Dolly, Stuttering Kate and Pearl Miller. Despite strenuous efforts by Mayor Cuddy, Thomas Mackie, and the Mounties, to eliminate them, the "bordellos" flourished during the construction booms of 1912 and 1913. Nose Hill overlooked the coulee in which the "settlement" lay, and was, surprisingly, a favourite Sunday picnic spot for the citizens of Calgary and their families. Thomas Wilson of Banff, the son of Tom Wilson who discovered Lake Louise and Emerald Lake, was taking a business course in Calgary. One Sunday afternoon, he was strolling around the hills with a camera, and, blissfully unconscious of the area's reputation, took a photograph of "Bawdy House Road", which had four large three-story houses and looked quite respectable. On continuing his stroll through the settlement, he noticed many young women around, and thought he had found a girls' school! So he asked a group of the "girls" to pose for him, got a rude awakening, and fled in embarrassment. During the first World War, 1914-1918, the Canadian Army took over several downtown stores in Calgary and turned them into barracks. There were many drinking saloons nearby. The Nose Creek area was too far away to compete with the facilities offered, and the houses there gradually emptied and were torn down. The photograph taken by Thomas Wilson is now in the Glenbow Museum, and has been chosen as the inside cover photo by James Gray for his book, "Red Lights on the Prairies."

The first hostelry on the Edmonton Trail north of Fort Calgary was the Dickson-Stephenson Stopping Place, not far from Airdrie. The Stopping Place catered for travellers from about the 1870's until 1900. John Dickson owned it first, and then Johnson Stevenson obtained title to it on December 9, 1895. He had fought in the Riel Rebellion and came home with a wounded lung. He was the Postmaster from 1900-1903. The Nose Creek Historical Society unveiled a plaque on October 25, 1981, to commemorate the Edmonton Trail and the Dickson-Stephenson Stopping Place.

On August 28, 1886, a stage coach on the Edmonton Trail was attacked and robbed by two masked highwaymen, just like the Wild West movies! There were three passengers, and they lost a total of $435, a considerable sum in the 1880's. Three mail bags were stolen as well. So the old Edmonton Trail had its share of excitement.

The Indians and the pioneer settlers dreaded the prairie fires that could whip across miles of unprotected land, burning all the grass and destroying any farm buildings that lay in the path of the fire. There were several disastrous fires in the winter of 1877-1878, that burned all the grass of the Blackfoot hunting grounds, driving the buffalo far to the south and east, and causing much hardship among the Indians. A more recent occurrence, on January 24, 1944, was the fire that started in a smoldering pile of straw in Silver Springs, and, whipped by strong westerly winds, raced eastward over the prairie and then over Nose Hill, until it was stopped by Nose Creek. It burned grassland, feed granaries, stock, homes and dairy buildings in its path. A still more recent and much smaller fire, in April 1987, was the one that destroyed the grass on the east side of Nose Hill and threatened to engulf the houses in Huntington Hills.

Acknowledgement

I would like to acknowledge the help given by Mr. C. Redvers Perry of the Nose Hill Creek Historical Society, who has kindly loaned much useful resource material.

References

Aramant, Robert 1983 *The Tipi-rings of Nose Hill.* The Calgary Field Naturalists' Society. Paper on file, Archaeological Survey of Alberta, Edmonton.
Calgary Herald Article, March 13, 1897.
Van Dyke, Stan and Sally Stewart 1985 *Hawkwood Site (EgPm 179).*

A Multi-component Prehistoric Campsite on Nose Hill. Archaeological
Survey of Alberta, Edmonton.
Reeves, Brian 1979 *Final Report, Historical Resources Inventory and
Assessment, Nose Hill Park.* Archaeological Survey of Alberta,
Edmonton.
Rogers, James ca. 1964 *Archaeology of Nose Hill.* M.A. Thesis.
University of Alberta at Calgary.
Wilks, Stephen 1963 *One Day's Journey.* (out of print)

Further Reading

Community Members 1960 *The Nose Creek Story.* Nose Creek
Historical Society.
Cunnicliffe, Richard 1969 *Calgary — In Sandstone.* Historical Society
of Alberta, Calgary.
Glover, Richard 1962 *David Thompson's Narrative.* The Champlain
Society, Toronto, Canada.
Gray, James H. 1971 *Red Lights on the Prairies.* MacMillan of
Canada, Toronto, Ontario.
Helgason, Gail 1987 *The First Albertans.* Lone Pine Publishing,
Edmonton, Alberta.
MacEwan, Grant 1958 *Fifty Mighty Men.* Modern Press, Saskatoon,
Saskatchewan.
Macoun, John 1922 *Autobiography of John Macoun.* Second Edition
(Revised) 1979. Ottawa Field Naturalists' Club, Ottawa, Ontario.
Perry, C. Redvers:
1960 *Historical Map of Nose Creek.*
1968 *The Nose Hill Spring.*
1978 *The Prairie Fires, 1878-1930's.*
1980 *The Sandstone Quarry Winch.*
1981 *The Hay Trails from 1875-1930's.*
1986 *Tribute to the Surveyors.*
All the booklets were sponsored by the Nose Creek Historical Society.

Habitats

Gordon Kerr

Various habitats, or communities, where the flowering plants, animals and birds may be found, have been identified. These are:

Grasslands

The grasslands of Nose Hill are representative of the "mixed prairie" that once covered all of Alberta's prairie regions except the southeastern corner. This is not a true prairie, where the grasses may grow to a height of 1.5 to 2.5 metres, but a grassland of medium grasses.

Typical of the grasses found on Nose Hill are Blue Grama Grass, June Grass, Spear Grass and Sweetgrass. Richardson Ground Squirrels and Meadow Voles may be found in this habitat. In winter flocks of Snow Buntings may be found on the hill. In the spring and fall Horned Larks are one of the most common birds on the hill. Both the Vesper Sparrow and the Savannah Sparrow may be found. Above the hill Red-tailed Hawks, Swainson's Hawks and American Kestrels may be seen, hunting the small mammals and insects of the hill.

South-facing Slopes

These slopes are covered with the grasses of the "mixed prairie", and to a lesser extent some of the shrubs from the shrub communities. The difference between these south-facing communities and these same communities elsewhere is that these slopes are somewhat drier.

Typical of the plants found on the south-facing slopes are: Prairie Crocus, Golden Bean, Yellow Umbrella Plant and Moss Phlox. Richardson Ground Squirrels are the most common mammals and Meadow Voles may also be found. Meadowlarks may be seen, singing from fence posts, in the grasslands of the south-facing slopes.

Ravines

Erosion from the waters of melting snow has cut into the slopes of Nose Hill, forming ravines. Small communities of "mixed prairie", shrubs and Aspens may be found on these slopes, which have many different exposures to the sun and wind. Each one of these exposures has a slightly different amount of the sun's heat, length of day and moisture, resulting sometimes in different plants, but almost always different flowering dates. The location of the winter snowdrifts is important.

Some of the large ravines have been named, for example Porcupine Valley; this ravine runs east and west. Here the characteristic plant of the north-facing slope is the moisture-loving Willow. The south-facing slope has been disturbed and one of the plants found here is the Kentucky Bluegrass. Porcupine, White-tailed Hare and Richardson Pocket Gopher may be seen in these ravines. House Wrens, Common Crows and Black-billed Magpies nest in the Willow thickets of the ravines. The latter two may be seen anywhere on the hill.

Shrub Communities

Shrubs are found wherever there is slightly more moisture than is required for the Aspen groves. This occurs most often on the slopes of ravines, away from the direct midday sun.

Typical shrubs found on Nose Hill are: Western Snowberry, Wolf Willow, Saskatoon and Chokecherry. White-tailed Hare and Meadow Voles are found in the shrub communities. American Robins, Clay-coloured Sparrows and Chipping Sparrows may be found, flying between this community and the grasslands.

Aspen Groves

These are one of the most characteristic features of Nose Hill and give shelter to a wide variety of wild life and wildflowers. Some of the birds that find shelter in the groves are: Great Horned Owls, Black-billed Magpies, American Robins, Common Starlings, Clay-coloured Sparrows and Song Sparrows. Some of the mammals that find shelter in the groves are: Deer, White-tailed Hare, Prairie Long-tailed Weasels and Meadow Voles. Some of the plants that grow in this habitat are Yellow Pea Vine, American Vetch, Star-flowered Solomon's Seal, Western Canada Violet and Buckbrush.

The additional moisture allows the Aspen trees to form groves. Aspen reproduce by root suckers, rarely, if ever, from seed; this results in the individual groves arising from the same tree. This gives these groves their characteristic shape, high in the centre and tapering down to the new, smaller plants on the outside.

Disturbed Areas

These include the gravel pits, abandoned fields, and areas of extreme overuse or overgrazing. Typical plants of the abandoned fields are: Canada Thistle, Blue Bur, Russian Pigweed and Stinkweed. The gravel pits attract the Rock Wren; this is the only place in Calgary where it may be found.

Springy Areas

There are several springy areas at the head of some of the ravines. There is one marshy area close to 53rd Street N.W. A typical plant of these damp areas is Silverweed.

Introduction to Plants   Beryl Hallworth

There are over 200 flowering plants on Nose Hill, and these are classified as Dicots (Dicotyledons) and Monocots (Monocotyledons). Dicots are plants that have seeds with 2 "seed-leaves" when they germinate; these seed-leaves are called cotyledons. The flowers usually have 5 petals or 4 petals, and the veins in the leaves are usually in the form of a net — spread out all over the leaf. Most of our familiar plants are Dicots, like Roses, Buttercups, Geraniums and Asters.

Monocots have seeds that possess 1 seed-leaf, or cotyledon, and usually their leaves have parallel veins. The flowering parts are usually in 3's. This arrangement is very clear in the Lily, which has 3 sepals and 3 petals (all alike) and 6 stamens, with 3 carpels (these form the fruit). Very many "bulb" plants belong to the Monocots, for example Lilies and Orchids. Grasses are also Monocots.

There are many plants that have no flowers — these are Ferns, Lichens, Mosses and Mushrooms. They usually reproduce by means of spores.

Plants can also be classified another way — into Vasculars and Non-Vasculars. A Vascular plant has conducting tissue in its stem — wood vessels to conduct water, and phloem vessels to conduct the food. These 2 types of vessels occur together as "Vascular bundles" running through the stem. These can be seen in Celery stems; the "strings" are the Vascular bundles. The veins in a leaf are also Vascular bundles. Flowering plants and Ferns are Vasculars, and Lichens, Mosses and Mushrooms are Non-Vasculars.

Glossary

The following glossary defines, pictorially, commonly used terms relating to all plants and also defines special terms used in describing grasses.

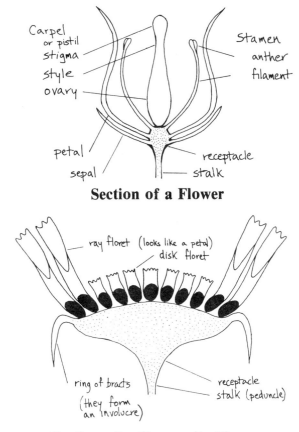

Section of a Flower

Section of a Composite Flower

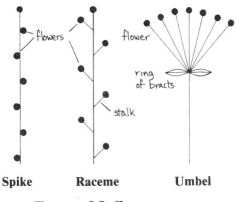

| Spike | Raceme | Umbel |

Types of Inflorescence

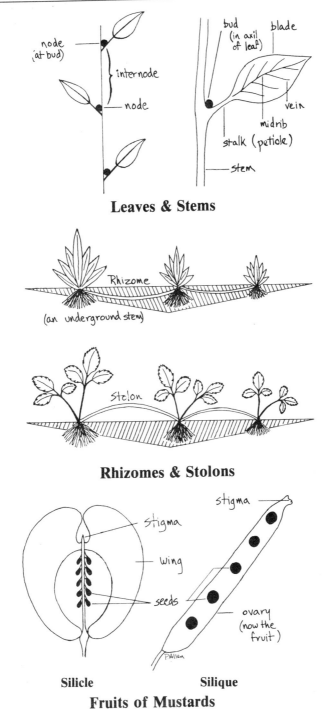

Leaves & Stems

Rhizomes & Stolons

Silicle   Silique
Fruits of Mustards

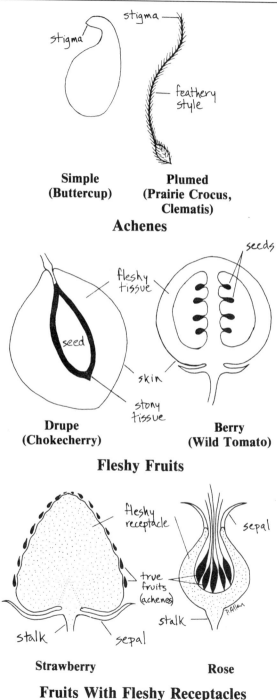

**Simple
(Buttercup)**

**Plumed
(Prairie Crocus,
Clematis)**

Achenes

**Drupe
(Chokecherry)**

**Berry
(Wild Tomato)**

Fleshy Fruits

Strawberry

Rose

Fruits With Fleshy Receptacles

Grasses

Panicle
A raceme of racemes; a flowering head of grass, a collection of spikelets.

Spikelet
The flowering unit of a panicle. The spikelet consists of two glumes which enclose one or more florets.

Floret
2 bracts, the lemma and palea, enclosing the flower (pistil and stamens).

Awn
A slender bristle; in grasses usually a continuation of the midvein of the glumes or lemmas.

Flowering Plants Other Than Grasses

Beryl Hallworth
Gordon Kerr

Flowering Periods

The flowering plant descriptions of the plants on Nose Hill have been divided into 4 periods, or seasons. These are periods when one could expect to find certain plants in flower. These are:

a. Early Spring — March 21 to May 6
b. Spring — May 7 to June 21
c. Summer — June 22 to August 7
d. Late Summer — August 8 to September 30

The descriptions of the plants are arranged so that all the plants from a certain period are together. Within this grouping the plants located in the same habitat are grouped together.

Therefore, by going to the hill on a specific date, and by going to a particular habitat, one should be able to determine from a limited number of descriptions the names of the plant from a limited list.

Each description:
a. explains the main features of the plant,
b. lists the habitat(s) in which the plant may be found,
c. notes any special features of the plant,
d. gives the scientific name of the plant and the plant family,
e. notes any special features of the plant's family.

Plants In Flower In Early Spring

Aspen Groves

Aspen
Populus tremuloides

The Aspen groves on Nose Hill are one of the most attractive and characteristic features of the hill; in addition they shelter a wide variety of wildlife. They are lovely in the spring when the young green leaves appear and also in the fall when the leaves turn yellow.

Aspens can reach a height of 30 metres, but this is never achieved on Nose Hill. The flowers are in drooping catkins, with the male and female flowers on separate trees. The bark is smooth, greenish-grey or almost whitish when young, becoming furrowed and dark as the trees mature. The leaves are a delicate green, and are roundish in shape, with a very slender flattened leaf stalk. This allows the leaves to flutter in any slight breeze, giving rise to the name "Trembling Aspen".

This tree belongs to the Willow family, Salicaceae; and the scientific name is *Populus tremuloides.*

Each Aspen grove arises from a single tree, spreading by underground suckers; the younger trees are clones of the original tree and are genetically identical. This explains why all the trees in a grove come into leaf at the same time, and turn yellow at the same time. It also explains the characteristic rounded shape of the grove, with the oldest trees in the centre and the younger ones at the edges.

Grasslands

Prairie Crocus *Anemone patens*

This beautiful flower is one of the joys of Spring. It appears when the warm sun and longer days provide sufficient heat in the ground. Its purple flowers are always a welcome sight. The plants are erect, 1 to 3 dm tall, and are protected from the cold winds by a covering of soft silky hairs. The flowers are 2 to 4 cm long and are rarely nearly white. In the fall, after the ground is cold, if there is a warm spell a few of these plants will respond as if Spring had come, and flower.

The Prairie Crocus is abundant in the grasslands, on the south-facing slopes, and bordering shrub communities throughout the area.

It is often called the "wind flower" and is an Anemone, not a Crocus (the Greek word for wind is "Anemos"). The purple "petals" are really coloured sepals — the flower does not have petals. There are numerous yellow stamens. After fertilization the fruits appear — these are delicate little plumed fruits that are dispersed by the wind. Any leaves associated with a flower are called "bracts", and there are always three on the flower-stem a little way below the flower; these look like leaves. The leaves appear later.

The Prairie Crocus, or *Anemone patens,* belongs to the Buttercup family, Ranunculaceae. This family always has five petals, when present, and 5 sepals. This flower is the floral emblem of Manitoba.

Moss Phlox (Plate 3) *Phlox hoodii*

This flower appears soon after the Prairie Crocus, but is not so easily noticed, because the flowers are much smaller (about 10 mm across and 8-10 mm long). The five petals are usually white but may be pale blue. This tufted, mat-forming plant grows very close to the ground; the awl-shaped leaves are very small (10-18 mm long) and moss-like, hence the common name. This small plant can have a tap root up to 45 dm long and may live up to 100 years old.

Moss Phlox is common on the south-facing slopes and in the grasslands throughout the area.

The scientific name, *Phlox hoodii,* is historically interesting because its name dates back to the John Franklin expeditions. In 1821, John Richardson, a member of the expedition, found this flower in the Northwest Territories (then, Prince Rupert's Land) and carefully preserved it. When Richardson returned to England he named the little flower in memory of his friend Robert Hood, who had been murdered by an Iroquois voyageur.

Moss Phlox belongs to the Phlox family, Polemoniaceae. In this family the five united petals are usually shaped like a funnel.

Bladderpod   *Lesquerella arenosa*

This short-lived, slender plant can be ascending or prostrate, with the delicate stems 0.1-2.5 dm long. The petals are yellow, tinged with red or purple, and are about 7 mm long. Each of the many small flowers has four petals in the shape of a Greek cross. The fruits are little pods, round in shape, hence the common name; the slender leaves are narrow to oval.

Bladderpod is fairly common in the grasslands and on the south-facing slopes.

This plant belongs to the Mustard family, with the scientific name of Cruciferae (cross-bearer), relating to the four petals. All members of this family have similar flowers making it quite easy to identify them. *Lesquerella arenosa* is its scientific name.

Early Cinquefoil (Plate 8)   *Potentilla concinna*

This low-growing plant is generally less than 1 dm high. It blooms from early April till the third week of June. It has attractive yellow flowers with 5 petals, 5 sepals, and, like all other members of the Cinquefoil group, it has 5 tiny "leaves" between the sepals; these are called bractlets. There are from 2 to 5 flowers on each plant and these flowers are 10-15 mm across. The leaves are palmately divided into 5 smaller leaflets like the fingers of a hand. These are covered with white hairs on the undersurface.

This plant is fairly common in the grasslands and on the south-facing slopes.

The flowers of the Cinquefoil and the Buttercup are very similar; the presence of small bracts between the sepals is an easy way to distinguish the Cinquefoil, as the Buttercup does not have these.

The Cinquefoils belong to the Rosaceae family which have flower parts in fives. The common name "Cinquefoil", however, refers to the fact that several of these plants possess leaves divided into 5 parts. The scientific name for the plant is *Potentilla concinna.*

Early Blue Violet (Plate 6)   *Viola adunca*
This Violet is often found in bloom at the same time as the Moss Phlox. This small tufted plant may be standing erect or may be spreading; the stems are 40 to 150 mm long. It has a pretty little blue or purple flower with the typical heart-shaped leaves, and it often colonizes disturbed ground. the flower itself is 8 to 15 mm long and is very interesting; it has five petals; one of them has a backward-pointing spur, with two stamens extending into it. These stamens are unique because they bear nectar glands as well as pollen. They are hooked — *"aduncus"* is the Latin named for "hooked". The fruit is a capsule that splits into three parts and produces many seeds.

This plant is common on the grassland slopes.

The Early Blue Violet, or *Viola adunca,* belongs to the Violet family, Violaceae.

All Violets produce two kinds of flowers, the showy ones we see in the spring and, later, curious little "closed flowers". These never open at all and are self-fertilizing, a kind of insurance in case the showy flowers do not get fertilized! They are called "cleistogamous" flowers.

Shrub Communities

Bebb's Willow   *Salix bebbiana*
This is a common prairie Willow, a shrub 1-5 metres high. The flowers, which bloom very early in the spring, are in the form of catkins; these are clusters of minute flowers which can be either male or female. The male ones are the familiar "pussy willows" which become yellow, covered with pollen. The catkins may contain 200-300 very tiny flowers, each consisting of a bract bearing 2 stamens. The female catkins are quite different — the tiny flowers are made up of a bract and a green vase-shaped ovary, which becomes the fruit. The male and female flowers are found on different shrubs. The leaves are usually oval and grow alternately up the twig.

This Willow is found in the shrub communities and moist grasslands on Nose Hill, with other Willows.

The Willow family is Salicaceae, and the Bebb's Willow is *Salix bebbiana.* Although adapted for pollination by the wind, the Willow is often pollinated by bees.

Plants In Flower In Spring

Aspen Groves

Yellow Pea Vine or Vetchling   *Lathyrus ochroleucus*
This is an attractive perennial climbing plant; climbing by means of
tendrils which are found at the tips of the leaves. The leaves are made
up of 3 or 4 pairs of leaflets. At the base of each leaf are two large leaf-
like stipules; these are characteristic of Pea Vines. The slender climbing
stems can grow to about 1 metre tall. The plant has pale yellow flowers
with the familiar "pea" pattern: a large standard petal at the back, two
petals forming wings, and two petals below, joined to form a keel. The
stamens, usually 10, are found inside the keel. The fruit is a legume,
that is, a pod opening along two sides.

The Vetchling is found growing in the shelter of the Aspen groves.

Lathyrus ochroleucus is the scientific name; the species name
"ochroleucus" meaning yellow. It is a member of the Leguminosae or
"Pea" family which includes Peas, Beans, Lupines and Loco-weeds.

Disturbed Areas

Hound's-Tongue   *Cynoglossum officinale*
Hounds's-tongue is a large coarse plant, 4-8 dm tall. The flowers are
reddish-purple, bell-like and grow in loose panicles. They have 5 sepals,
5 petals, 5 stamens, and the fruit consists of four nutlets, which are very
prickly. The sepals, like the petals, are united at the base. Each nutlet
supposedly looks like the tongue of a hound, hence the common name.
The whole plant is covered with soft hairs. The leaves are lanceolate;
the lower ones have leaf-stalks and the upper ones clasp the stem.

Hound's-tongue is found in disturbed areas, and in the grasslands on
the slopes of Nose Hill.

It is a biennial, that is, it flowers in its second year and then dies.

The soft hairs covering the plant are characteristic of Boraginaceae, the
Borage family, to which it belongs. The scientific name is *Cynoglossum
officinale*. The generic name, *Cynoglossum,* comes from two Greek
words meaning "dog" and "tongue". The species name, *"officinale",*
means "a plant which was used in medicine".

Flixweed or Tansy Mustard   *Descurainia sophia*
Flixweed is a tall, erect plant, with many branches, averaging 3-10 dm
high, although some reach 20 dm high. It looks greyish-green because
the whole plant is covered with fine hairs. The flowers are quite small,

only 2-4 mm across, are yellowish-white and are grouped into racemes. It belongs to the Mustard family, Cruciferae; the flowers in this family all look alike. They have 4 sepals, 4 petals (in the shape of a Greek cross), 6 stamens and 2 carpels which form the fruit. The fruit is either a long thin pod or a round one. Flixweed has the former, called a silique. The leaves are finely divided into long narrow segments.

Flixweed is one of the commoner weeds in Canada; it flourishes in the disturbed ground on Nose Hill.

Common Dandelion   *Taraxacum officinale*

The Dandelion is a very familiar weed of disturbed areas, and is, unfortunately, all too common on Nose Hill. It has a very interesting "flower" which is made up of hundreds of strap-like florets. Each of these florets is essentially a single flower; with 5 yellow petals linked together to form the "strap", which becomes a tube at the base; inside the tube are the 5 stamens, the pistil is found below the strap. The calyx, instead of being composed of the usual green sepals, consists of a *"pappus"* of hairs. When the flower has been fertilized, the pistil forms the long narrow fruit and the pappus becomes the familiar "parachute", which is so readily dispersed by the wind. The leaves are toothed in a characteristic way, coarsely toothed with triangular lobes.

The plant was called "Dent-de-lion" (tooth of the lion) and this has been corrupted into Dandelion. The young tender leaves can be used as a salad and the tap-root can be used for making "dandelion coffee".

The scientific name is *Taraxacum officinale,* and it belongs to the family Compositae: all its members have a "composite" head of flowers, surrounded by 1-several rings of bracts, called an involucre.

Stinkweed or Pennycress   *Thlaspi arvense*

This common annual is 2-5 dm high and has tiny white flowers. It belongs to the Mustard family and has the characteristic 4 petals, 4 sepals, 6 stamens and 2 carpels, which form the pistil. The lower leaves have leaf-stalks but those higher up the stem have none; they clasp the stem and are sometimes toothed. When the flowers have been fertilized the pistil turns into a flat, rounded silicle, broadly winged and deeply notched at the apex. The whole plant turns yellow soon after fruiting.

Stinkweed is a true weed and spreads very rapidly in the disturbed areas where it is found on Nose Hill. The seeds are very numerous and can remain viable for a long time.

It has, unfortunately, an unpleasant odour, hence the common name.

The scientific name for this member of the Cruciferae family is *Thlaspi arvense, arvense* pertaining to fields or cultivated land.

Grasslands

Canada Anemone   *Anemone canadensis*

This is a striking plant, 2-7 dm tall, with large white flowers; the flower
has no petals, but has 5 showy white sepals which are 10-20 mm long,
and there are numerous stamens and carpels. It has attractive palmate
leaves with long leaf stalks. The blades are strongly veined. These
plants are perennials.

Anemones are found on the grasslands of the south-facing slopes, in
the Aspen groves, and also in the shrub communities.

All Anemones have coloured sepals taking the place of petals; this is
not uncommon in the Buttercup family, Ranunculaceae, to which they
belong. The scientific name of this Anemone is, appropriately,
Anemone canadensis.

Fairy Candelabra   *Androsace septentrionalis*

The rather fanciful name comes from the dainty habit of this plant; it is
25-200 mm high, with a neat little basal rosette of leaves, and the
flowers are very tiny. They are borne in dainty little umbels. Each
flower has 5 green sepals, 5 white petals and 5 stamens. The fruit is a
capsule which bursts open when ripe.

The Fairy Candelabra plants are found in the grassland areas of Nose
Hill and on the slopes. They are sometimes found as weeds in neglected
gardens.

The scientific name is *Androsace septentrionalis* — a long name for a
tiny plant. They belong to Primulaceae, the Primrose family, and are
annual plants. The species name, *"septentrionalis"*, is the Latin word
for "northern". It is sometimes seen on old maps.

Small-leaved Pussytoes   *Antennaria parvifolia*

This unusual name, Pussytoes, comes from the flower-head, which
consists of about 5 small flower-heads grouped together in a bunch, so
that they look rather like a kitten's paw. Each small flower-head is
surrounded by a ring of bracts, forming an involucre, which protects
the flower-head in bud. These bracts are stiff and "everlasting". The
heads may be male (staminate), producing only pollen, or female
(pistillate), producing the pistils, which turn into fruits. These are small
plants, 10-25 cm tall, and spread rapidly by means of stolons (creeping
stems), forming quite extensive mats. They are perennial, and have
greyish, spatulate (spoon-shaped) leaves in a rosette.

They are found on the grasslands of Nose Hill, especially on the south-
facing slopes.

The scientific name for this plant is *Antennaria parvifolia,* the species name, *parvifolia,* meaning "small-leaved". It is a member of the Compositae or Dandelion family, and has the characteristic flower-heads of this family.

Reflexed Rock Cress   *Arabis holboellii*

There are several different plants called "Rock Cress", and they are all similar, with a rosette of basal leaves, a straight stiff stem, and small leaves arranged alternately up the stem. This one is 2-7 dm tall. As they belong to the Mustard family, Cruciferae, they all have the typical flower, 4 sepals, 4 petals, 6 stamens and 2 carpels joined together to form the pistil. The petals are pinkish to white and are 5-10 mm long. When the flower has been fertilized the pistil turns into the fruit, a long thin pod called a silique, which splits open when ripe. These siliques, when ripe, point down, that is, they are reflexed.

The Reflexed Rock Cress is found on the grasslands of the south-facing slopes.

The scientific name of this member of the Cruciferae family is *Arabis holboellii.* The 4 petals are thought to look like a cross, hence the name Cruciferae.

Buffalo Bean or Ground Plum   *Astragalus crassicarpus*

The Buffalo Bean is one of the Milk Vetches: there are 25 of these plants in Alberta, and some of them are extremely difficult to distinguish from one another. Fortunately, the Buffalo Bean is quite distinctive; the flowers tend to grow in a ring round the plant, and from a distance look like a wreath of flowers about 7 dm across. The flowers themselves are fairly distinctive — they are typical "pea" flowers and are yellowish white with a purplish keel. Each Pea flower has 5 petals: a large standard petal at the back, 2 wing petals at the sides and 2 keel petals joined together at the bottom. These enclose the 10 stamens and the pod-shaped carpels, which develop into the fruit. The fruit of the Buffalo Bean is exceptional; the "pod" develops into a large, pink swollen fruit 20 mm in diameter, which looks rather like a plum, hence the common name, Ground Plum. The fruits lie on the ground below the stems and leaves; these "plums" are edible. The numerous leaves have 17-25 narrow to oblong leaflets. The dry "plums" of the previous year are usually found near the plant, and sometimes in piles stashed away by Ground Squirrels.

These plants are found on the grasslands of the south-facing slopes of Nose Hill — they are typical prairie plants.

Astragalus crassicarpus is a member of the Leguminosae or Pea family.

Chickweed   *Cerastium arvense*

This is a dainty, straggly plant with thin stems, which often forms mats, bearing numerous relatively large white flowers. These have 5 petals, about 15 mm long, cleft at the tip, with 5 sepals and 10 stamens. There are 5 carpels, which when fertilized, turn into a cylindric capsule. This splits open when ripe, releasing the reddish-brown seeds. The narrow leaves are 10-40 mm long and grow in pairs up the stems.

Chickweed is found on the grasslands and on the slopes of Nose Hill.

The scientific name for this plant is *Cerastium arvense* and it belongs to the Pink family, Caryophyllaceae. The common Chickweed of our gardens is also a member of this family.

Pale Comandra   *Comandra umbellata* var. *pallida*

This rather inconspicuous plant is only 1.5-4 dm tall, with small greenish-white flowers, 2-4 mm long, so it is easily overlooked. These flowers have no petals — there are 5 greenish-white sepals and 5 stamens; the carpel turns into a dry inconspicuous fruit.

It is quite a common prairie plant and is found on the dry south-facing slopes.

The scientific name of this plant is quite interesting; it is *Comandra umbellata* var. *pallida,* and has no widely used English name. The variety name *"pallida"* means pale. Pale Comandra belongs to an interesting family, the Sandalwood family, Santalaceae, which is mostly a sub-tropical family.

Wild Strawberry   *Fragaria virginiana* var. *glauca*

The Wild Strawberry is easily recognized because of its resemblance to the cultivated variety; it is 0.5-2.5 dm tall, with several white flowers about 20 mm across. There are 5 petals, 5 sepals, about 20 stamens and numerous carpels; the petals are longer than the sepals. The leaves have long petioles arising from the base of the plant, with three coarsely toothed leaflets. The fruit is a red juicy edible so-called "berry" with numerous minute seed-like achenes scattered over it.

Wild Strawberry is found in the Aspen groves and shrub communities on the hill, and flowers from mid-May to early July.

The scientific name for this plant is *Fragaria virginiana* var. *glauca,* and it is a member of the Rosaceae family. One method by which Straw-berries reproduce is by long creeping runners or stolons, which root at the nodes and produce new plants.

Three-flowered Avens   *Geum triflorum*

This plant has distinctive purplish flowers; there are usually three of these growing together, hence the common name; this also explains the scientific name of *Geum triflorum.* This plant is 2 to 4 dm tall and the individual flowers are 12 to 20 mm across; the reddish-purple colour of the flowers comes from the sepals and the little bractlets between them — there are five of each, like the Cinquefoil. The petals are cream-coloured and are practically hidden by the sepals. The flowers are nodding, but when they are fertilized they turn into a tuft of fruits with feathery plumes. These fruit-stalks become erect and so the plumed fruits can be dispersed by the winds.

This plant is common on the south-facing grassland slopes, on the slopes of the ravines and at the edges of the Aspen groves.

There are two other common names for this plant which refer to the fruits: Prairie Smoke and Old Man's Whiskers. The leaves of the Three-flowered Avens appear very early in the spring, long before the flowers, and are quite characteristic — they have several leaflets arranged in the shape of a feather — they are pinnate; *"pinna"* is the Latin name for a feather.

Three-flowered Avens belongs to the Rose family, Rosaceae. In this family the flower parts, petals and sepals and bracts are usually five in number, with numerous stamens.

Northern Hedysarum, Mackenzie's Hedysarum
Hedysarum boreale var. *mackenzii*

This common perennial has many long, 2-6 dm, flowering stalks growing from a common base. It has very colourful deep purple flowers in a short raceme. The flower has the typical pea-shape, although the keel tip is angular rather than rounded. The leaves are compound with 9-13 oblong leaflets. The fruit-pods are called loments; these are long, thin and jointed; this jointing or constriction between the seeds is unique to the genus Hedysarum, in the Pea family.

The Northern Hedysarum is found on the grassland and south-facing slopes throughout the Natural Area.

This plant was called Mackenzie's Hedysarum after Alexander Mackenzie, the explorer; the old scientific name was *Hedysarum mackenzii*. The new scientific name is *Hedysarum boreale* var. *mackenzii, boreale* meaning northern. It is a member of the Pea or Leguminosae family.

American Hedysarum,
or Alpine Hedysarum *Hedysarum alpinum*

This is a handsome erect plant, 200 to 700 mm high, with a long raceme of pinkish or reddish-purple flowers. The flower has five petals: a large standard, two wing petals and two keel petals, typical of the pea family. Inside the keel are the ten stamens and the pistil. The pistil turns into the pod

Alpine Hedysarum
(Hedysarum alpinum)

or loment when mature. Characteristic of this genus of the pea family are the constructions of the pod between the seeds. The compound leaf has 15-21 leaflets which are broadly oblong.

Alpine Hedysarum is found in the grasslands and Aspen groves on Nose Hill.

This plant, like many of the legumes, is readily eaten by grazing animals.

The Hedysarum belongs to the Leguminosae family, and its scientific name is *Hedyarum alpinum* var. *americanum*. The species name, *"alpinum"*, seems to be a misnomer as it is most often found at lower elevations, on the prairies.

Incised Puccoon   *Lithospermum incisum*

A medium-sized, 1-5 dm tall perennial, with small, golden-yellow flowers, growing near the top of the plant. The flowers consist of a long tube with 5 wavy-margined "incised" petals, 10-30 mm long, and about 15 mm across. There are several stems with many narrow pointed leaves about 50 mm long, both with a somewhat rough texture. Later in the season smaller flowers, often without petals, appear; these are self-fertilized and produce most of the fruits. The fruits are very hard, ivory-white nutlets.

The Puccoon is found in the grasslands on the hill and flowers in the Spring.

The scientific name is *Lithospermum incisum:* the genus name is from the Greek *"lithos"* meaning "stone" and *"sperm"* meaning "seed", referring to the small hard fruits.

Early Yellow Locoweed   *Oxytropis sericea* var. *spicata*

A robust, tufted plant with leafless flowering stems 40-300 mm long. The pale yellow flowers grow in a dense spike-like raceme, with 6-27 flowers per spike. There are 5 sepals, 5 petals, 10 stamens and two carpels; these flowers resemble the familiar garden pea, which belongs to the same family. The fruit is a short, hairy, pea-like pod. The leaves all grow from the tufted base, are compound, with 11-15 leaflets, and are covered with fine silvery hairs. The plant may be poisonous in locations where it can concentrate harmful salts, like selenium, that affect the nervous systems of cattle. "Loco" is the Spanish word for "crazy".

Locoweed grows in the grasslands on Nose Hill and flowers in the spring.

The Early Yellow Locoweed is a member of the Pea family, Leguminosae, and the scientific name is *Oxytropis sericea* var. *spicata*.

Heart-Leaved Buttercup   *Ranunculus cardiophyllus*

This plant is a typical Buttercup — the yellow flowers have 5 petals, which are oval-shaped and very shiny, 5 sepals and numerous yellow stamens. These flowers are 10-20 mm across and there can be several on each plant. They are erect plants, little branched, 1-4 dm high. The lower or basal leaves have stalks and are round to oval, sometimes lobed. The tiny green fruits each have a little beak.

This is a common plant of the south-facing slopes of Nose Hill, which is especially interesting as it is not common even in its normal habitat, which is moist meadow and open woods.

Buttercups are usually found in damp places, and have the scientific name of *Ranunculus*. *"Rana"* means "frog", which is also found in damp places. This particular Buttercup with its heart-shaped leaves is *Ranunculus cardiophyllus*. *"Cardio"* means "heart" and *"phyllos"* means a leaf.

Prairie Buttercup   *Ranunculus rhomboideus*

This plant blooms in May and is an attractive Buttercup, with yellow flowers, so it is a welcome sight in the spring. It is a low perennial, 1-2 dm high, with hairy stems. The basal leaves are rhombic in shape and have leaf stalks; the stem leaves are quite different: they have no leaf stalks and are divided into 3-5 lobes. The flower is rather distinctive because the 5 sepals are yellowish with a purple tinge and the 5 petals are much longer than the sepals. There are numerous stamens, and the carpels are in a round "head".

The Prairie Buttercup grows on the south-facing slopes of Nose Hill.

The scientific name is *Ranunculus rhomboideus*. The species name, *"rhomboideus"*, refers to the rhombic-shaped leaves. It belongs to the Buttercup family, Ranunculaceae.

Prairie Groundsel   *Senecio canus*

This is quite a striking plant because of the bright yellow rays of the flowers and the long basal leaves, which are covered with white hairs. The flower-heads are composed of yellow disk flowers in the centre and a ring of bright yellow ray flowers surrounding them. These ray flowers attract insects for pollination. The plant is 1-4 dm tall with one or more stems and is a perennial. The basal leaves are more or less tufted, are 10-80 mm long, and the white hairs give them a velvety appearance. The stem leaves have no leaf stalks or petioles (they are sessile) and become smaller up the stem.

These plants grow in the grasslands on the slopes of Nose Hill.

Some of the Alberta Groundsels are difficult to distinguish (there are 18 species), but this one should present few problems.

Senecio canus belongs to the Dandelion family, Compositae, and has the characteristic flower-head of disk and ray flowers. It is the earliest-flowering plant with both disk and ray flowers on the hill. Some members of the family, like the Dandelion itself, have only ray flowers.

Golden Bean (Plate 7)   *Thermopsis rhombifolia*

This is a medium-sized plant, 1-4 dm high, and, when in bloom, forms large golden patches on Nose Hill — quite a striking sight. As the name implies, it belongs to the Pea and Bean family, and the flower has the characteristic shape. The flower is bright yellow and 10-20 mm long, and there are five petals. The large one at the back is called the standard, the ones at the sides are called the wings and the two in front are joined to form the keel. The ten stamens are hidden inside the keel. After fertilization a "bean pod" appears. This is quite distinctive because it is always curved into a bow shape. The leaf is divided into three oval or elliptical leaflets and has 2 rhombic-shaped stipules.

This plant is abundant on the grassland slopes, in the Aspen groves and in the shrub communities. It flowers from April 22 to June 24.

The fruit pod or legume contains several seeds and these are poisonous; they have caused **SEVERE SICKNESS** in children.

The Golden Bean belongs to the Leguminosae family, named after the fruit, which is called a legume. The scientific name for this plant is *Thermopsis rhombifolia.*

Yellow Prairie Violet   *Viola nuttallii*

This is an attractive yellow Violet, 5-10 cm high. The leafy stems arise from a stout rootstock and the leaves are lanceolate with long leaf-stalks. The flower has 5 petals and 5 sepals; the petals are interesting — they are bright yellow with purple veins at the base, and one of them has a backward-pointing spur which is rather short. There are 5 stamens; two of these extend into the spur and possess nectar glands. There are 3 carpels joined together; when fertilized these form a capsule, which splits into 3 parts when ripe, and releases the seeds.

Yellow Prairie Violets are found on the grassy south-facing slopes, in the Aspen groves and in the shrub communities.

This Violet has two kinds of flowers — the showy ones produced in late Spring, and, later on, curious little closed flowers, that never open and are self-fertilized. These are usually found low-down on the plant and are not very easy to see. They are called "cleistogamous" flowers.

The scientific name for this Violet is *Viola nuttallii* and is named after a well-known British botanist named Thomas Nuttall. It belongs to the Violet family, Violaceae.

Heart-leaved Alexanders or Meadow Parsnip   *Zizia aptera*

These two common names give us two definite characteristics of this plant, namely, that the basal leaves are heart-shaped and that the plant belongs to the Parsnip or Carrot Family. In this family the flowers are arranged in an umbel, like an upside-down umbrella. The individual flowers are very small and are bright yellow. There are 5 yellow petals (the sepals are usually lacking), and 5 stamens, with 2 carpels joined together, in the centre of the flower. When fertilized the carpels turn into the fruit, which splits into 2; each part has one seed inside it. The plants are perennials and are 2-6 dm high.

Heart-leaved Alexanders are found on the grassy south-facing slopes and in the shrub communities.

The scientific name is *Zizia aptera,* and the plant is a member of the Umbelliferae family.

Prairie Onion   *Allium textile*

This Monocot is not a conspicuous plant — it is only 0.5-3 dm tall, but its white flowers are a welcome sight in late May. The Prairie Onion grows from a bulb, producing long narrow leaves with a flowering stalk in the centre. At the top of the flowering stalk is a cluster of white flowers. Each flower consists of 3 sepals and 3 petals, all exactly alike, with 6 stamens and an ovary in the centre. This ovary consists of 3 carpels joined together, which later turns into the fruit. This is a small capsule, splitting into 3 parts, and releasing the small black seeds.

It is fairly common on the south-facing grassland slopes of Nose Hill.

The scientific name is *Allium textile,* and the plant belongs to the Lily family, Liliaceae.

Star-flowered Solomon's Seal
(Plate 4)   *Smilacina stellata*

This plant is a Monocot with pretty white flowers, and certainly fits the description "star-flowered", because the small white flowers have 6 white "tepals", just like a star. Tepals refer to the sepals and petals when they are exactly alike; the outer ring represents sepals, and the inner ring, petals.

Prairie Onion
(Allium textile)

There are 6 stamens and 3 carpels joined together. The fruit is a good-sized berry, green at first, then striped with deep purple, and finally black. The zigzagged stems are 2-6 dm high, with clasping, overlapping, bright green stalkless leaves.

Star-flowered Solomon's Seal is found in the grasslands and Aspen groves on the hill.

The second part of the common name is a misnomer — it is not at all like the true Solomon's Seal, which has pendulous, bell-shaped flowers. The plant spreads by means of numerous rhizomes, just like Lily of the Valley.

All three plants belong to the Lily family, Liliaceae; the scientific name for the Star-flowered Solomon's Seal is *Smilacina stellata*. *"Stella"* is the Latin name for "star".

White Camas   *Zygadenus elegans*

White Camas (Zygadenus elegans)

This tall, graceful Monocot is a member of the Lily family, Liliaceae, and the greenish-white flowers have their flower-parts in 3's. There are 3 petals and 3 sepals, all exactly alike, with a gland at the base of each. There are 6 stamens, and the fruit is a 3-lobed capsule, formed from the 3 carpels. The plant arises from a bulb and has linear leaves, and in the centre is a tall flowering stalk, bearing numerous flowers, arranged in a raceme.

The White Camas is found on the north-facing and south-facing grassland slopes, and in the shrub communities.

The scientific name for this plant is *Zygadenus elegans* — the species name means "elegant", and aptly describes it.

Blue-eyed Grass   *Sisyrinchium montanum*

The common name is a misnomer. It is an Iris, not a grass, although the leaves are certainly grass-like. Like a grass, it is a Monocot. The stems are 1-5 dm tall. It has attractive blue flowers; these have the typical monocot structure with all the parts in 3's. There are 3 pointed sepals and 3 petals, all exactly alike, and deep blue in colour. The name "tepals" is often given to these; they are characteristic of the Lily family, but rather rare in the Iris family. The Garden Iris looks different. There are 6 stamens, and 3 carpels in the centre of the flower — these carpels are joined together and turn into a capsule, which splits into 3.

Blue-eyed Grass is found in the grasslands on Nose Hill.

The scientific name of this plant is *Sisyrinchium montanum,* and the Iris family is Iridaceae.

Ravine

Western Canada Violet (Plate 8)   *Viola canadensis* var. *rugulosa*

These handsome plants grow to 1-4 dm in height, and bear attractive white flowers; these flowers are found in the axils of the upper leaves, and have 5 sepals and 5 white petals with a yellow base. Occasionally the petals are violet-coloured. One of these petals has a backward-pointing spur — this is characteristic of Violet flowers. Inside this spur are 2 of the 5 stamens. There are 3 carpels joined together, and when fertilized these form the fruit — a capsule which splits into 3 to release the seeds.

Western Canada Violets are found in the slightly damper ravine sides and bottoms, and shrub communities.

These plants produce stolons, so that they spread easily and make large colonies, always a welcome sight.

This Violet has the scientific name *Viola canadensis* var. *rugulosa,* and it belongs to the Violet family, Violaceae.

Shrub Communities

Saskatoon   *Amelanchier alnifolia*

This shrub is often called Serviceberry, or Juneberry, and is usually 1-4 metres high. It often forms colonies because it spreads by low branches, which when in contact with earth produce new plants complete with roots and shoots. These branches are called stolons. The shrub bears white flowers in a dense spike-like raceme. All the parts of the flower are in fives or multiples of five; the petals are quite characteristic. They are white, thin and 6-10 mm long. There are 20 stamens. The carpels turn into the familiar Saskatoon fruits — shaped like tiny apples, purple in colour. They are edible, and the Plains Indians used them for food — either in pemmican or dried in the sun and pressed into cakes for winter use. These fruits make excellent pies. The leaves grow alternately up the twigs and are usually oval with no teeth.

These shrubs may be found in the shrub communities, on the open prairie or along the sides of the ravines.

The scientific name for the Saskatoon is *Amelanchier alnifolia, alnifolia* meaning "leaves like the Alder". It belongs to the Rose family, Rosaceae. Many of the plants in this family produce edible fruits such as Strawberries, Choke Cherries, and Raspberries. All have the characteristic five petals.

Red Osier Dogwood   *Cornus stolonifera*

This is quite a handsome shrub; it grows 1-3 metres high and bears clusters of small white flowers. The clusters are 20-50 mm across. These produce large white berries which are not edible. The twigs are deep red and are quite conspicuous in the winter, giving the name "Red Osier" to the shrub. The leaves are in pairs on the twigs, usually oval and without teeth. They turn bright red in the fall.

The Red Osier Dogwood is found in the shrub communities and in the Aspen groves on Nose Hill and is fairly common. The name "Dogwood" has no connection with dogs: in Britain the wood was used to make "dags", or pegs, and so the shrub was called Dagwood, which became Dogwood.

The scientific name is *Cornus stolonifera, "stolonifera"* meaning that it produces "stolons" or lower branches which will root in the ground away from the main plant. It belongs to the Dogwood or Cornaceae family, which also includes the small Bunchberry plant.

Wolf Willow or Silverberry   *Elaeagnus commutata*

This is one of the common shrubs on Nose Hill and it is quite distinctive, because the leaves are greyish and have a wavy outline. The flowers are also distinctive because they are tubular, up to 1.5 cm long and are yellow inside, but silver-grey outside, with a strong scent. The first sign of flowering is this scent which you can smell from 2 metres or more away. The fruits are also unusual because they are silvery round "berries" with a large stone inside. These stones have 8 well-marked ridges and are rather decorative. They were used by Indian women to make necklaces.

Wolf Willow is found in the shrub communities and in the grasslands.

This shrub is found in large colonies because it spreads both underground and by stolons. These are horizontal branches from the base of the shrub which, when they touch the ground, produce roots and form new plants.

The scientific name for the Wolf Willow is *Elaeagnus commutata,* and it belongs to the family Elaeagnaceae. It is, of course, not a Willow!

Choke Cherry   *Prunus virginiana*

This is a slender shrub or, sometimes, a small tree, and can reach 8 metres in height, though not on Nose Hill. The bark is dark and the branches are reddish-brown. The flowers grow in racemes, and have 5 sepals (soon shed), 5 white petals and 20 stamens. The fruits are 1-seeded drupes, just like pea-sized plums. These fruits are black or reddish-purple and have a sharp taste, which has given the shrub the common name Choke Cherry. The leaves are usually ovate (egg-shaped) and are toothed. There are 2 tiny "ears" on the leaf stalks, called auricles, a distinguishing feature of Choke Cherry leaves.

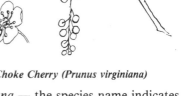

Choke Cherry is found in the shrub communities and in the grasslands.

Choke Cherry (Prunus virginiana)

The scientific name is *Prunus virginiana* — the species name indicates that it was found in the State of Virginia. The shrub belongs to the Rose family, Rosaceae; some familiar members of the family are cherries, plums and apples.

Wild Gooseberry   *Ribes oxyacanthoides*

Wild Gooseberry is a small shrub 3-6 dm high, with rather straggling stems; there are spines at the nodes, and the internodes are often covered with bristles. The flowers are cream-coloured and tubular — there are 5 petals, 5 sepals and 5 stamens, all attached to a tubular base, and 2 carpels. These carpels turn into true berries, reddish-purple in colour, which are edible. The leaves grow alternately up the stem, have 3-5 lobes and are rather hairy.

The Wild Gooseberries are found in the shrub communities, and in the shelter of rocks.

The scientific name for the shrub is *Ribes oxyacanthoides*. The Greek word *"acanthus"* means "a spine". Gooseberries belong to the Currant family, Grossulariaceae.

Common Wild Rose or Wood's Rose (Plate 5)   *Rosa woodsii*

The Rose is one of the loveliest flowers and is deservedly popular; when we see our first rose we feel that summer will soon be here. It is a thorny shrub 0.5-1.5 m high. The flower has 5 petals, pink or sometimes white, and 5 sepals; there are numerous yellow stamens, and in the centre of the flower is a globe-shaped or oval structure which becomes red and fleshy to form the fruit, the familiar rose-hip, which is very rich in

Vitamin C. The stems have scattered thorns, and the leaves have 5-9 leaflets.

It is found in the shrub communities, and in grasslands, and often grows in large colonies.

There are 3 Alberta roses, and these frequently form hybrids. The most common one on Nose Hill is Wood's Rose, *Rosa woodsii,* which belongs to the family Rosaceae. The Prickly Rose, *Rosa acicularis,* is Alberta's floral emblem.

South-facing Slopes

Yellow Umbrella Plant   *Eriogonum flavum*

This is a conspicuous plant, 3-4 dm tall, with umbels of bright yellow flower-heads. Each head of flowers (the umbel) is surrounded by a ring of bracts which look like leaves; each small flower has 6 yellow sepals, no petals and 9 stamens. Although the individual flowers are small there are so many of them that they make a good splash of colour. The leaves arise from the base of the plant, are thick, have leaf stalks and are densely covered with white hairs. The stalks supporting the umbels are 1-3 dm tall.

These plants thrive in a semi-desert environment, and are found on the dry south-facing slopes.

The common name is Yellow Umbrella Plant, but it does not belong to the Carrot family, Umbelliferae, as one might expect, but to the Buckwheat family, Polygonaceae. The scientific name is *Eriogonum flavum, "flavus"* meaning "yellow".

Smooth Blue Beard-tongue   *Penstemon nitidus*

This is one of the loveliest prairie plants; it has striking deep-blue flowers and attractive leaves — it certainly adds to the beauty of the prairie in late spring. The deep blue flowers grow in tall racemes and each flower has a bract underneath it. There are 5 sepals and 5 petals; each petal is lipped — there are 2 parts, an upper lip and a lower lip. These extend into a tube, to which the 5 stamens are attached inside. The leaves are oval-shaped, blue-green, rather pointed and are arranged alternately up the stem; these stems are 1-3 dm tall.

The plants are found on the dry south-facing slopes of Nose Hill.

The name "Beard-tongue" comes from the fact that although the flower has 5 stamens, the fifth one is sterile and has a hairy tip or "beard". This lies in the "throat", or tubular part of the flower, and has a fanciful resemblance to a "tongue".

All the Beard-tongues (there are 10 in Alberta) belong to the Figwort or Snapdragon family, Scrophulariaceae. The scientific name for our plant is *Penstemon nitidus* which refers to the stamens because *"penstemon"* means "5 stamens".

Springy Areas

Silverweed or Silver-leaf Potentilla   *Potentilla anserina*

This plant lives up to its name of "Silver-leaf" because the undersurfaces of the leaflets are covered with silky hairs, and are quite distinctive. The flowers are bright yellow; they have 5 green sepals below the petals, have numerous stamens (20-25), and numerous carpels, which turn into dry achenes. The leaves arise from the base of the plant, and are pinnate (feather-shaped) with 7-21 leaflets.

Silverweed is found in springy areas on Nose Hill.

The plant produces stolons, like a Strawberry; these produce roots and leaves at the nodes, forming separate little plants.

Silverweed has the scientific name *Potentilla anserina,* and is a member of the Rose family, Rosaceae. Linnaeus named this plant *"anserina"* because, in his native Sweden, flocks of geese frequented marshes, where he found this flower. The Goose tribe is called Anserini.

It is sometimes difficult to distinguish between a Buttercup, Ranunculaceae, and a Cinquefoil, Rosaceae, because the flowers look alike, but while both have 5 green sepals below the flower, the Cinquefoils also have 5 small leaf-like bractlets in between the sepals, and this is very characteristic.

Plants In Flower In Summer

Aspen Groves

American Vetch   *Vicia americana*

Vetches and Pea Vines can easily be distinguished from other plants belonging to the Pea Family because they possess tendrils. The climbing stems of the American Vetch are 3-10 dm high and bear leaves with 8-14 leaflets; the end leaflets have been modified into tendrils. These enable the plant to climb over other plants. Each reddish-purple flower has the usual pea-like structure: 5 sepals, 5 petals — the large standard at the back, 2 wing petals and 2 keel petals joined together. There are 10 stamens, and the ovary is pod-like.

American Vetch plants are found in the Aspen groves and shrub communities.

The scientific name of this plant is *Vicia americana* and it is a member of the Leguminosae family. The only other genus in the Pea family on Nose Hill, having tendrils, is *Lathyrus,* the Pea Vine or Vetchling.

Disturbed Areas

Canada Thistle   *Cirsium arvense*

This is a tall plant with stems 3-10 dm in height with very prickly leaves. The flower-heads are pink, purple or occasionally white, and consist of numerous tubular florets. These little florets can be either all male (with stamens), or, in another flower, all female (with ovaries). Only the latter form the fluffy fruits. These little "parachute" fruits are carried by the wind and are effectively dispersed in this manner.

This plant is a "noxious" weed, and is found in disturbed areas and in the grassland communities, where it spreads underground forming large colonies.

The name "Canada Thistle" is a misnomer: this ubiquitous and unwelcome weed was introduced from Eurasia. It deserves the term "noxious" because it spreads rapidly by means of rhizomes, as well as by fruits, making it very difficult to eradicate.

The scientific name is *Cirsium arvense* and it belongs to the Dandelion family, Compositae.

Common Peppergrass   *Lepidium densiflorum*

This is an annual, 2-5 dm tall, with a single erect stem, and many small, white flowers in numerous racemes. The flowers have the characteristics of the Mustard family, to which it belongs, with 4 petals, 4 sepals, 6 stamens and 2 carpels. The carpels form the fruit, which is called a silicle. This is oval and 2-3.5 mm long. The lower leaves are deeply toothed, with very short, grey-green hairs; the upper leaves are slightly toothed.

Peppergrass is found in the disturbed areas of the hill and blooms in the summer.

This plant belongs to the Mustard family, Cruciferae, and the scientific name is *Lepidium densiflorum;* the species name refers to the dense racemes of flowers.

Bluebur or Beggar-ticks   *Lappula squarrosa*

The common name of this plant is very appropriate; it is certainly blue, like Forget-me-nots (which belong to the same family), and the fruit is burred or prickly. The plant is 1-5 dm tall and the flowers are quite small, but attractive; with 5 sepals, 5 petals and 5 stamens. The petals are joined to form a tube, with 5 lobes at the top. The leaves are linear and are not prickly; they are reduced in size upwards on the stem. The fruit consists of prickly nutlets; these prickles are barbed and cling to clothing or the coats of animals. In this way the fruits are dispersed.

This plant is a weed and is found on disturbed ground all over Nose Hill, showing that this form of dispersal must be quite effective.

The scientific name is *Lappula squarrosa,* an older species name being *echinata;* the plant belongs to the Borage family, Boraginaceae. *Echinata* means "spiny".

Grasslands

Common Yarrow or Milfoil *Achillea millefolium*

Yarrow is a very common prairie plant, 3-7 dm tall, with several flat-topped flower-heads. Each flower-head is made up of numerous, tiny (6 mm across), separate flower heads. These have 5 little white (sometimes pinkish) ray-flowers, and 10-30 yellowish disk flowers. Both have stamens and a pistil. Milfoil has many very finely divided, fern-like alternating leaves.

This plant is found in the grasslands of Nose Hill and it blooms from mid-June to late August.

The scientific name is *Achillea millefolium;* this is interesting because *"Achillea"* comes from the name of the Greek warrior Achilles, who is supposed to have used the plant to make an ointment to cure his soldiers after the battle of Troy. The species name, *"millefolium"*, means "a thousand leaves". The plant belongs to the Dandelion family, Compositae. It is an aromatic herb which, since medieval times, has been used to cure bleeding and has many common names such as "Woundwort" and "Carpenters Weed" to illustrate this healing factor.

False Dandelion *Agoseris glauca*

This common name is certainly appropriate because the flower does resemble the Dandelion flower, with hundreds of yellow ray florets — each "petal" is really a small separate flower, but a closer look will show that the real Dandelion flower-head has 2 rows of leaf-like bracts around the head; the outer row is bent backwards and looks rather untidy. In the False Dandelion the bracts overlap one another in several rows. The leaves are quite different from Dandelion leaves in that they are not pinnately lobed, while those of the Dandelion are.

The tiny individual flowers (or florets) are interesting; each consists of 5 petals joined together to form a "strap" which becomes a tube at the base. Inside this tube are the 5 stamens. The fruit is just like that of the Dandelion — a small brown achene with a white "parachute" or *pappus,* which is dispersed by the wind.

The False Dandelion is found on the grasslands of Nose Hill.

The scientific name for the False Dandelion is *Agoseris glauca* and it belongs to the Compositae or Dandelion family. This family, because of the many separate flowers per head (and hence fruits), is one of the most prolific and successful in the plant kingdom.

Cut-leaved Anemone or Wind-flower   *Anemone multifida*

Like all Anemones, there are no petals; the colour comes from the 5 sepals of each flower; there are 1-4 flowers on each plant, 12-18 mm across. There are several stamens and carpels in the centre of each flower. The carpels, when fertilized, turn into tiny fruits called achenes. The stems and leaves are covered with fine hairs and the leaves are much divided. The plants are 1.5-5 dm tall.

This plant is quite common on Nose Hill, and, like the Canada Anemone, is found on the grasslands of the south-facing slopes and in the shrub communities. It tends to be found in drier sites.

An interesting feature of this plant is that the flowers are often of different colours — they may be cream, reddish, or purple.

The scientific name is *Anemone multifida;* this is appropriate because *"multifida"* means "much divided", and refers to the leaves. The genus name Anemone comes from the Greek word *"anemos"* which means "wind".

Tufted Fleabane   *Erigeron caespitosus*

There are 24 Fleabanes in Alberta, and many of these are very difficult to recognize. Fortunately, the one that grows on Nose Hill is fairly common and not too difficult to identify. It has blueish, pinkish or white flowers, 20-40 mm across. It has several stems which are 1-2.5 dm high, curved at the base, and then grow erect. The leaves at the base of the plant are rather spoon-shaped, 25-75 mm long, with the stalk; the stem-leaves are much reduced and without stalks. As the plant belongs to the Dandelion family, the flower heads consist of hundreds of tiny ray and disk flowers, which turn into fruits with tiny "parachutes".

The Tufted Fleabane is common in the grasslands, and flowers in the summer.

The scientific name is *Erigeron caespitosus,* the species name meaning "growing in a tufted fashion".

Small-flowered Rocket   *Erysimum inconspicuum*

This is a showy, perennial Mustard, with stiff, branched stems, 3-6 dm tall. Each stem has a terminal raceme of tiny (inconspicuous) yellow flowers. As in all Mustards it has 4 petals, in the form of a Greek cross, 4 sepals, 6 stamens and 2 carpels. These carpels, when fertilized, form the fruit, a long thin pod called a silicle, which bursts open, when ripe, to release the seeds. The leaves are long and narrow with tiny branched hairs.

Small-flowered Rocket is found in the grasslands on Nose Hill from late May to early August.

Mustards belong to the Cruciferae family. The name Cruciferae comes from 2 Latin words, *"crux"* meaning "cross" and *"fera"* meaning "to carry", referring to the 4 petals. This is a very clear distinguishing feature of all the Mustards, making it easy to assign the plant to its family. However, there are many Mustards, and it is often difficult to distinguish between them. The scientific name of this one is *Erysimum inconspicuum,* and the small yellow flowers are rather inconspicuous, but there are so many that they give a show of colour.

Gaillardia or Brown-eyed Susan · *Gaillardia aristata*
Gaillardia is one of the most striking plants on the prairie, with very attractive, large, yellow flower heads. These are 45-65 mm across, and are made up of deep purple-brown disk-flowers in the centre, and large, yellow, petal-like, ray flowers on the outside. Each plant is 3-6 dm tall, with hairy, greyish-green, alternate leaves. The brown disk flowers give rise to the name Brown-eyed Susan.

It is found in the grasslands of Nose Hill and blooms from early June to late July.

The plant belongs to the Dandelion family, Compositae, in which all the members have these "composite" flower heads. The scientific name of the plant is *Gaillardia aristata.*

Northern Bedstraw · *Galium boreale*
This Bedstraw is a typical prairie plant, and is also found in woodlands and roadsides. It is an erect plant, 3-6 dm high, with masses of tiny (2 mm across) white flowers; these flowers are quite distinctive because they have only 4 petals, and this is unusual. There are no sepals, but there are 4 stamens and 2 carpels; the carpels turn into 2 little nutlets. The flowers are slightly fragrant. A closely-related species is called "Sweet-scented Bedstraw". The leaves are in whorls of 4, they are narrow, and 2-5 cm long.

This Bedstraw is found in the grasslands and on the south-facing slopes.

The common name, "Bedstraw", arises from the time when mattresses were stuffed with straw, and these plants were added to make them smell "sweet".

The scientific name for the Northern Bedstraw is *Galium boreale* — the species is named after Boreas, the God of the North Wind.

The Sweet-scented Bedstraw is *Galium triflorum,* which is found in moist woods. It is not found on the hill.

Sticky Purple Geranium (Plate 6)   *Geranium viscosissimum*

This Geranium is quite a handsome plant; it grows to a height of 2-9 dm with large purple flowers which are typical of the Geranium, or Cranesbill family, with 5 sepals (these are glandular and hairy), 5 large petals and 5 stamens; there are 5 carpels which are joined together and continue upward in the shape of a "cranes-bill". The fruits are in the form of long-beaked dry capsules, splitting lengthwise into 5 divisions. It has distinctive leaves divided into 5 or 7 parts, which are densely hairy and are often glandular, like the leaf stalks. This accounts for the name Sticky Purple Geranium.

The plants are found in ravines, in the shrub communities and in the grasslands.

The scientific name is *Geranium viscosissimum* — the species name means "sticky" which is very appropriate. It belongs to the Geranium family, Geraniaceae.

Wild Blue Flax   *Linum lewissii*

This is a dainty plant with pretty, pale blue, saucer-shaped flowers scattered on the upper stems; it is 2-8 dm tall. There are 5 sepals and 5

petals; the flower blooms for one day only: on the second day the petals fall to the ground. There are also 5 stamens and 5 carpels. These carpels turn into a capsule which bursts open when ripe, to liberate 10 seeds. There are numerous, narrow leaves, 10-20 mm long.

Wild Blue Flax is common in the grasslands of Nose Hill and blooms from early June to September.

The scientific name is *Linum lewisii,* and it is a close relative of the Common Flax, *Linum usitatissimum;* the Common Flax is grown for linseed oil (squeezed from the seeds) and for the stem-fibres, which are used to make linen. It is not found on the hill. Both plants belong to the family Linaceae.

Wild Blue Flax (Linum lewisii)

Puccoon or Woolly Gromwell   *Lithospermum ruderale*

This is a conspicuous plant, with numerous branches, forming a large clump about 6 dm across and up to 5 dm high. Although the plant itself is conspicuous, the tubular yellow flowers are not — they are only

5-8 mm long and tend to be hidden by the very numerous leaves. Each flower has 5 green sepals and 5 yellowish-white petals. The fruits or nutlets are white, smooth, shiny and hard, like little stones. The leaves are linear or lanceolate and are crowded on the stems.

The plants are found on the south-facing slopes of Nose Hill.

The scientific name *Lithospermum ruderale* is interesting because *"litho-spermum"* means "stone seed". The whole plant is hairy; this is typical of plants belonging to the Borage family, Boraginaceae.

Wild Bergamot or Horse Mint   *Monarda fistulosa* var. *menthaefolia*

The Bergamot is an outstanding flower on the prairie slopes of Nose Hill; it has a large reddish-purple flower-head consisting of very many separate flowers. It is a perennial, 3-7 dm tall. As the plants grow in large colonies, they produce a blaze of colour in late summer. In fact, the plants look as if they had escaped from a garden, but they are native to North America. Each flower-head is surrounded by bracts and is made up of very numerous separate flowers; these heads are 38-64 mm across. Because the flowers are so crowded the plant may be mistaken for a member of the Dandelion family, Compositae. Each of the separate flowers has a cup-like calyx made of sepals joined together, and 5 petals, each has 2 "lips"; these indicate that the plant probably belongs to the Mint family; the rest of the flower is made up of 2 stamens and 2 carpels; the latter produce 4 little nutlets.

Wild Bergamot is common in the grasslands of Nose Hill and blooms in late summer.

The scientific name is *Monarda fistulosa* var. *menthaefolia,* and it belongs to the Mint family, Labiatae, (*"labium"* means "lip").

Purple Prairie Clover   *Petalostemon purpureum*

This plant is quite distinctive, because the flowers are a deep rich purple colour; they grow in a dense cylindrical head, with the individual flowers opening from the bottom upwards. These flowers are not typical of the Pea family although they have the same basic structure. The 5 petals are almost the same shape and size and there is no keel. The fruit pods (legumes) are very small and form a cylindrical head. The leaves are divided into 3-5 small, narrow leaflets. The plant grows from 2-8 dm high.

It is found in the grasslands of Nose Hill.

The scientific name is *Petalostemon purpureum,* and it belongs to the Pea family, Leguminosae.

Nodding Onion   *Allium cernuum*

A low, 1-5 dm tall, slender Monocot that looks and smells like a common garden Onion. The small pale-lavender to white flowers, about 6 mm across, are lily-shaped, and there are several in a loose, nodding cluster at the top of the main flowering stalk. There are 3 petals and 3 sepals all exactly alike (these are sometimes called "tepals", and they are 5-7 mm long). There are 6 stamens, and 3 carpels. The latter are joined together in the centre of the flower. When fertilized, they turn into the fruit, which is a small capsule, splitting into 3 valves, to release several black seeds. There are several leaves which are long, narrow, ridged and arching at the top.

This plant is fairly common in the grasslands of the south-facing slopes.

The scientific name for this Onion is *Allium cernuum* and it is a member of the Lily or Liliaceae family. Like many members of the Lily family, this plant grows from a bulb, in this case a slender one with a fibrous outer coat.

Western Wood Lily (Plate 7)   *Lilium philadelphicum* var. *andinum*

This is one of the loveliest flowers on the hill, with rich orange-red petals and sepals. As in many Monocots, these are exactly alike. These "tepals" have purplish black spots on the inside, and are quite distinctive. There are 6 stamens, and 3 carpels joined together, in the centre. These carpels produce the fruit, which is a capsule. This flower is typical of the Lily family, Liliaceae, with all its parts in 3's. The plant arises from a bulb, which is also fairly characteristic of the family. The leaves are long and narrow, and the upper ones are whorled.

The Western Wood Lily is found on the north-facing grassland slope, in sunny clearings in Aspen groves, and occasionally in shrub communities.

The scientific name of this plant is *Lilium philadelphicum* var. *andinum,* and it is the floral emblem of the Province of Saskatchewan. It is sometimes called the "Tiger Lily", but this is a misnomer — the real Tiger Lily is quite different.

Ravine Slopes

Spreading Dogbane or Indian Hemp   *Apocynum androsaemifolium*

The Dogbane is a tall, branching plant, 2-10 dm high; it is quite common in the summer. The flowers are not very conspicuous but, when examined more closely, they are quite attractive; they are little pink or pink-striped bells, 6-9 mm long, massed together in cymes. These flowers each have 5 sepals, 5 petals, 5 stamens (joined to the petals), and 2 carpels. The carpels become the fruits, which are quite distinctive — they are long, 80-120 mm, thin pods which burst open to release many seeds, each with a tuft of silky hairs for wind dispersal.

It is found in ravines, where it forms part of the shrub community. It is also found on the dry south-facing slopes.

The plant is called "Indian Hemp", because the tough fibres in the stem can be soaked, removed and woven into rope, and these were used by the Indian women.

The scientific name is *Apocynum androsaemifolium,* and it belongs to the Apocynaceae family. The species name *"androsaemifolium"* means that the leaves resemble those of *Androsace,* a plant in the Primrose family, Primulaceae.

Fireweed or Great Willow-herb   *Epilobium angustifolium*

Fireweed is indeed well-named, because it is often found after a timber-burn; the burnt-over ground becomes covered with these tall handsome plants, from 1.3-15.0 dm high, producing long racemes of reddish-purple flowers. Each flower is 10-30 mm across, and has 4 petals — this is unusual, because most flowers have 3 or 5 petals. There are 8 stamens, and the fruit is a capsule with 4 valves. This capsule is again distinctive; it is very long, 40-100 mm, and is coloured deep red. When it bursts, it releases dozens of little seeds each with a tuft of white hairs. "Plumed" fruits are quite common, e.g. the Dandelions and Thistles, but plumed seeds are quite uncommon. The leaves are 15-200 mm long and 5-35 mm wide and have short stalks, or petioles.

Fireweed is quite common on some of the ravine slopes, forming spectacular sheets of purple in late summer.

The scientific name is *Epilobium angustifolium,* and the species name means "narrow-leaved". The alternate common name of Great Willow-herb comes from the fact that the leaves are like those of the Willow, lance-shaped. There are 16 different species of Willow-herb in Alberta, and they belong to the family Onagraceae, the Evening Primrose family.

Shrub Community

Shrubby Cinquefoil   *Potentilla fruticosa*

This is a small shrub, 3-10 dm high, which is quite common on Nose Hill. It branches freely, and the outer bark shreds easily, giving the plant a scruffy appearance. The shrub belongs to the Rose family, and the flower has the usual 5 petals and 5 sepals — the petals are yellow. There are 5 little green bracts alternating with the sepals; this is characteristic of the Cinquefoils and makes them easily distinguished from the Buttercup family. The leaves are divided into 5 parts (hence the name "Cinquefoil"), have a short stalk and are about 13 mm long.

This plant is found in the shrub communities and in the grasslands of Nose Hill.

The scientific name of the Shrubby Cinquefoil is *Potentilla fruticosa* — the species name *"fruticosa"* is the Latin name for "shrubby". There are 28 Cinquefoils in Alberta, and many of them are difficult to identify, but this is the only shrubby one.

Buckbrush   *Symphoricarpos occidentalis*

This shrub is very common on Nose Hill — it is the dominant plant in the green patches that clothe the ravines, and can be seen from a long way away. It grows up to 1 metre high, and forms large colonies, spreading by suckers. The pink flowers grow in clusters, with 5 petals, joined at the base to form a funnel-shaped tube. There are 5 stamens joined to the petals, and 1 carpel. The fruits are also in a cluster; they are round, greenish-white and fleshy. The oval leaves are numerous and are rather thick and leathery, with no teeth.

The scientific name is rather cumbersome — *Symphoricarpos occidentalis.* It belongs to the Honeysuckle Family, Caprifoliaceae; the species name *"occidentalis"* means "western" and is sometimes seen on old maps.

South-facing Slopes

Scarlet Mallow   *Sphaeralcea coccinea*

This is a striking prairie plant, with large reddish-orange flowers, and it is spread by rootstock, forming colonies. These make a welcome splash of colour. It is a perennial plant with a woody base and is found in dry places. The whole plant is covered with star-shaped hairs. The stems tend to grow close to the ground and then grow upwards; these decumbent stems are 1-3 dm long. The leaves are deeply divided into 2-5 parts. The flowers are 10-20 mm across, in a short spike; the five sepals are joined to form a cup and the five petals are yellowish-red or brick-red; they form a saucer shape. The numerous stamens form a little column in the centre of the flower, and there are ten carpels associated with them. These ten carpels are interesting: they are joined together and look like a little cheese with ten segments. They become the fruit when fertilized and each segment has a little seed inside it.

Scarlet Mallow is found on the dry south-facing slopes. The scientific name is *Sphaeralcea coccinea* and the plant belongs to the Mallow family, Malvaceae.

Plants In Flower In Late Summer

Grasslands

Pasture Sage   *Artemisia frigida*

This common prairie perennial is 1-4 dm tall, with a somewhat woody stem, and is often mat-forming. A member of the Dandelion family, it does not have ray flowers, only disk flowers; these are yellowish, with stamens and carpels, about 3 mm high. There are many flower heads, crowded in a leafy cluster. The leaves are silvery-hairy, alternate and finely dissected, feathery; different from most other Sages.

Pasture Sage is found in the grasslands and overgrazed areas of the hill.

The scientific name is *Artemisia frigida,* and it is a member of the Compositae family. The plant gives off a strong aromatic odour if bruised; as it is unpalatable to livestock it increases on overgrazed areas of Nose Hill.

Prairie Sage   *Artemisia ludoviciana*

This is a common Sage in Alberta and is very characeristic of our native prairie. The clumps of silvery-grey foliage form a striking background to the many colourful prairie flowers. It is a perennial plant which spreads by creeping rootstocks, forming patches; it is 3-6 dm tall. Sages are members of the Compositae family, but in this case there are only disk flowers. These are brownish, with both stamens and carpels. The flower heads are very small, 3-4 mm high, numerous in a narrow spike-like cluster. The stems and leaves are covered with very tiny, silvery hairs which give the plant its beautiful colour and velvety feel. The leaves are alternate, entire or somewhat toothed, 0.1-0.8 dm long.

Prairie Sage is found in the grasslands of Nose Hill and flowers in the late summer.

The scientific name for this plant is *Artemisia ludoviciana.* When rubbed between the fingers, this Sage, like most Sages, gives off a pleasant aromatic smell.

Smooth Aster   *Aster laevis*

This is a very common member of the Dandelion family, and is a rather handsome plant 4-10 dm tall. It has large flower heads, 25 mm across; this "head" is composed of 15-20 blue-purple ray flowers, and numerous yellow disk flowers. The lower leaves form a cluster at the base of the plant, and have stalks, while the upper leaves clasp the stem.

This Aster is common on the south-facing grassland slopes.

There are 21 Asters in Alberta. One of the most common is the Smooth Aster, *Aster laevis;* it is a member of the Compositae family.

Tufted White Prairie Aster   *Aster ericoides* ssp. *pansus*

This rather untidy plant generally has curved stems clustered together, which are rough-hairy, and 3-8 dm tall. This plant is a member of the Dandelion family with the flower heads composed of 2 types of florets. These flower heads are numerous, and are 12 mm across. There are

10-20 of the white outer ray florets, and numerous inner disk florets. The leaves are less than 25 mm long, are narrow, and are clustered on the stem of the plant.

This plant is found on the south-facing grassland slopes of Nose Hill.

There are several white Asters in Alberta, but the common one on the hill is *Aster ericoides* ssp. *pansus,* a member of the Compositae family.

Bluebell or Harebell   *Campanula rotundifolia*

Bluebells are one of the best-known flowering plants. There are three species native to Alberta, only one being found on the hill. The slender stems are 2-4 dm tall, with several blue, bell-shaped flowers, 12-18 mm long, on each stem. These flowers have 5 lobes, 5 stamens and one carpel; the stigma is conspicuous, with 3 lobes. The fruit is a short capsule, with many smooth seeds. The stem-leaves are numerous, linear and narrow, up to 8 cm long.

Bluebells are found in the grasslands of Nose Hill.

The scientific name is *Campanula rotundifolia,* and it is a member of the Campanulaceae family. This plant is native to both the Old World and the New World and is found in many different habitats, growing throughout the summer months. *"Campanula"* means "a bell".

Golden Aster   *Heterotheca villosa*

This is a perennial, with several spreading, almost creeping, stems, mostly 2-5 dm long. There are several flower heads, 25-50 mm across, each of which is composed of golden-yellow ray-flowers, which each have a carpel, and yellow disk flowers, which have both stamens and carpels. The bracts are overlapping, hairy and glandular. The many leaves are alternate, oblong to lance-shaped, hairy, greyish-green, and 20-50 mm long.

Although it is called the Golden Aster it is not a true Aster; these are rarely yellow.

Golden Aster is found in the grasslands of the south-facing slopes of Nose Hill.

The scientific name was *Chrysopsis villosa;* it has recently been changed to *Heterotheca villosa,* and the plant is a member of the Compositae family.

Wavy-leaved Thistle   *Cirsium undulatum*

This is a robust plant, 3-12 dm tall, with several deep-purple flower-heads; it is a native thistle. The flower heads, like those of all thistles, are composed of numerous, tubular flowers, surrounded by a ring of spiny bracts. The stems are covered with fine white hairs, as are the undersides of the leaves, which are coarsely toothed, and are very prickly.

These plants are found in the grasslands and sometimes in the disturbed areas of Nose Hill.

The scientific name for this plant is *Cirsium undulatum;* a very similar thistle, *Cirsium flodmanii,* is also found on the hill. In the latter plant the leaves at the base of the plant form a rosette of long pointed leaves with very few prickles. By the time the flowers are in bloom these basal leaves have disappeared, making the two plants hard to distinguish from one another. Both plants belong to the Dandelion family, Compositae.

Broomweed   *Gutierrezia sarothrae*

A medium-sized perennial, 2-4 dm tall, with numerous, erect, slender, brittle stems. This rather common member of the Dandelion family has many small yellow flower-heads, 0.3 cm across, which are clustered in flat-topped corymbs at the tops of the stems. There are no disk flowers and the yellow ray flowers have both stamens and carpels. The bracts surrounding the flower-heads are sticky and leathery. The leaves are alternate, very narrow and usually hairy, about 1-4 cm long.

This is a common plant on Nose Hill in the late summer in the grasslands.

Broomweed is a member of the Compositae family, and the scientific name is *Gutierrezia sarothrae*. The numerous, erect, stiff stems have suggested the common name, Broomweed. Because it is unpalatable to cattle it tends to increase in overgrazed areas, but makes a welcome splash of colour in the late fall.

Goldenrod   *Solidago*

There are a number of species of Goldenrod which are common on the hill. They are all perennials with slender, erect stems. The large inflorescence is composed of many small, yellow, composite flower-heads; the yellow ray-flowers have carpels, and the yellow disk-flowers have both stamens and carpels; both are fertile. The leaves are alternate, entire to toothed.

All the Goldenrods are found in the grasslands of the hill, and flower in the late Summer.

All are members of the Compositae or Dandelion family. The individual species on the hill are:

Solidago spathulata, formerly *decumbens,* which is 1-4 dm tall, somewhat reclining at the base; the inflorescence is cylindrical to oval in shape.

Solidago gigantea, which is 5-20 dm tall with the inflorescence in a broad pyramidal raceme.

Solidago missouriensis, 1-6 dm tall, with the inflorescence broadly rounded or flattened at the top. Individual flower-heads tend to grow on one side of the inflorescence, that is, they are "secund".

Further Reading

Cormack, R.G.H. 1967 *Wildflowers of Alberta.* The Queen's Printer, Edmonton

Looman, J. and K.F. Best 1979 *Budd's Flora.* Research Branch, Agriculture Canada, Publication 1662. Canadian Government Publishing Centre, Hull, Quebec

Moss, E.H. 1959 *Flora of Alberta.*

Packer, John J. 1983 *Flora of Alberta.* Second Edition. University of Toronto Press, Toronto, Ontario

Vance, F.R., J.R. Jowsey and J.S. McLean 1977 *Wildflowers Across the Prairies.* Western Producers Prairie Books, Saskatoon, Saskatchewan

Linda Cole
Catharine Osborne

Grasses

Introduction

Grasses are some of the most important plants in the world, because all the cereals are grasses — wheat, oats, maize (corn), and also rye, barley and rice. Some of these have been domesticated by man for thousands of years, for example a form of wheat was grown in the New Stone Age 5000 years ago.

Grasses are flowering plants; the flowers are pollinated by the wind, and so have no colourful petals or sepals to attract insects. The individual flowers (florets) are tiny and difficult to see. Only when they are in full bloom, with bright yellow stamens hanging out, is there any show of colour at all. Although the flowers are tiny, the Grass family is one of the most highly-evolved in the plant kingdom. The grasses are very successful, and form the dominant species in prairies, steppes and savannahs all over the world.

The Grass family is Poaceae, formerly Graminea, and all grasses are Monocots (Monocotyledons), producing only one cotyledon (seed leaf) when the seed germinates. Because it is such a large family, grasses are further divided into sub-families and tribes.

In grasses, the meristematic tissue (actively growing zone) is at the base of the leaf blade where it leaves the stem. This adaptation enables grass to continue growing from the base to regenerate itself following grazing (or lawn mowing).

Grasses of Nose Hill

Sweetgrass   *Hierochloe odorata*
Sweetgrass grows from long, creeping rhizomes. It may grow to 60 cm tall with a 10-15 cm long, open panicle. The panicle is pyramid-shaped with the florets tipping the ends of the drooping branches. This shape, together with the shining golden-yellow to papery brown, oval glumes enclosing the fruit, attract the eye as it is a decorative species.

Sweet Grass (Hierochloe odorata)

The Blue Grasses *(Poa)* could be confused with Sweetgrass but Sweetgrass has a distinct fragrance when dried. The Indians used Sweetgrass to make baskets and decorations.

Sweetgrass belongs to the Canary Grass Tribe (Phalarideae); it grows in wet sites and is never abundant. Look for it in the moist swales on the north side of Nose Hill.

June Grass
Koeleria macrantha

June Grass is a low perennial (to 50 cm), which stands erect rather than having a drooping head. The bluish-green, tufted leaf blades often catch the eye amid the Needle-and-Thread Grass with which it is associated.

The grass head is spike-like, 2 to 8 cm long, which appears dense in spring but at flowering time it extends and opens to show the discontinuous spikelets (5 mm long). From the spikelets hang the beautiful yellow anthers and the head temporarily assumes a pyramidal shape. Other aids to identification are the shining, silvery panicles and the lack of awns.

June Grass is never abundant, but it is a ubiquitous species which grows on a variety of soils and provides excellent forage. It is the only native member of its genus *(Koeleria)* in North America. June Grass belongs to the Oat Tribe (Aveneae).

Crested Wheatgrass
Agropyron pectiniforme

Crested Wheatgrass is a large, coarse bunchgrass with striking spikelets and leaf blades to 4 mm wide. The spikelets are 5 to 7 cm long and are composed of florets attached flatwise directly to the stem in a way reminiscent of a series of partly-finished, divergent crystals. The spike-like inflorescence is unlike any other species on Nose Hill as the native wheatgrasses are daintier with less coarse spikelets.

Crested Wheatgrass is a common component of reclamation seed-mixes and is commonly used with Alfalfa by the City of Calgary on many sites, including the area between Nose Hill and John Laurie Boulevard. The extensive root-mass can grow to a depth of 1.5 metres enabling this imported species to flourish under dry soil conditions.

The Wheatgrasses belong to the Barley Tribe (Hordeae), and the *Agropyron* genus contains Quackgrass *(Agropyron repens)*, a common invader of the home lawn.

Northern Awnless Brome   *Bromus inermis* ssp. *pumpellianus*
Smooth Brome   *Bromus inermis* ssp. *inermis*

These two species are being treated together as distinguishing them without a hand lens is very difficult. The first, Northern Awnless Brome, is a native of the Fescue Grasslands, while the second, Smooth Brome, is very common throughout Calgary as it is a component of land reclamation seed-mixes, having been introduced from Europe as a forage grass.

The heads appear large and compact with the pendulous spikelets falling on one side of the stem, contracted but not spike-like, when first encountered. On further examination, the heads are found to be composed of many individual branches each with many large spikelets. The florets overlap each other and have minute awns. The overall pattern is that of shingles on a roof (termed imbricate). The stalks may reach 1 metre high in favourable locations, while the grass blades are 5 to 12 mm wide, far wider than those of Rough Fescue with which it could be confused.

The two species of Brome hybridize and on Nose Hill may be found around the edges of the plateau as well as in other locations.

Bromegrasses belong to the Fescue Tribe (Festuceae), with the Bluegrasses and the Fescues.

Foxtail Barley   *Hordeum jubatum*

Foxtail Barley is a distinctive, tufted grass, like its cultivated counterpart, and is characterized by having dense clusters of flowing awns to 6 cm long which turn purple in the autumn. A common grass in disturbed places, Foxtail Barley grows in dense stands and is an early colonizer of waste areas.

Foxtail Barley has coarse stems and leaf blades which may be to 6 mm wide. The spikelets occur in sets of three at each node of the stem and are attached directly to it (sessile). Each fruit has four to eight of the characteristic, long, barbed awns which readily attach to animals and clothing. It is a short-lived perennial which does not spread by vegetative means but relies on its prolific seed production for regeneration.

Foxtail Barley is found in disturbed places across Nose Hill. It prefers moist sites and is often found in isolation on alkaline soils and gravelly areas where other grasses are less successful. Although it is a native species of Alberta, it is considered a weed as the sharp, barbed awns lower the quality of hay.

Kentucky Bluegrass *Poa pratensis*

Kentucky Bluegrass is a sod-forming grass which spreads quickly by rhizomes, which enable it to colonize open areas. Consequently the Bluegrasses are an important component of lawn seed-mixes.

Kentucky Bluegrass has an open, dainty panicle which may extend to 6 cm wide. The lower branches usually occur in whorls of five and thus the spikelets are not compressed, nor do they fall to one side of the stem.

A distinctive feature of the Bluegrass genus *(Poa)* is the keel, or boat-shaped tip at the end of each leaf blade. By running your finger along the leaf blade to the tip you can "break open" the keeled tip, thus you know you have a Bluegrass. The genus is a difficult one for botanists. However, its many members are widespread and provide valuable forage and lawn species due to the persistent rhizomes.

Kentucky Bluegrass is a member of the Fescue Tribe which also includes the Bromegrasses and the Fescues — all of which have many-flowered spikelets.

Parry Oat Grass *Danthonia parryi*

Parry Oat Grass grows in association with Rough Fescue in the Fescue Grasslands Ecoregion which encompasses Nose Hill. Parry Oat Grass forms large, tough tussocks from which the stout stems grow to 60 cm tall. The panicles are somewhat open, 2-4 cm long, with the appressed branches ascending rather than flowing or drooping. There are two florets per spikelet and each floret has a distinctive awn (1 cm long) which is bent at right angles to the floret. The papery glumes which enclose the floret may be up to 2 cm long and, along with the bent awn, provide another aid to identification.

Parry Oat Grass looks like a small version of its cultivated cousin, the Oat, and may be found across Nose Hill; both belong to the Oat Tribe (Aveneae).

Rough Fescue *Festuca scabrella*

Rough Fescue is a dominant native grass which gives its name to the Fescue Grass Ecoregion in which Nose Hill lies.

Rough Fescue is an erect (to 90 cm tall) dense tussock-grass which often has short rhizomes. Clumps of Rough Fescue have a bluish tinge, and the leaf blades are narrow and scabrous (rough). Run your finger along the leaf blade to feel the rough texture which will help to eliminate Blue-grass — a tribe member — when you're working on identification.

The panicle is narrow with branches occurring singly or in pairs. The spikelets have four to six florets, and these, like Smooth Brome, are imbricate (arranged like shingles on a roof).

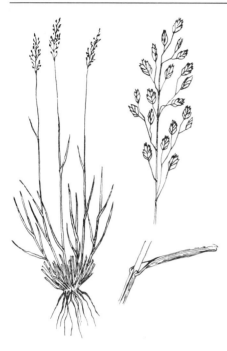

Rough Fescue (Festuca scabrella)

Rough Fescue is a dominant, native grass on Nose Hill and is the conspicuous grass occurring in many undisturbed habitats.

Rough Fescue belongs to the Fescue Tribe (Festuceae) along with the Bluegrasses and Bromegrasses.

Hair Grass, Tickle Grass
Agrostis scabra

Hair Grass leaf blades are short and dense (to 10 cm long). The plant is tufted, which emphasizes the large, delicate panicle which is often to 20 cm long and half as wide, atop a 50 cm high stem. Hair Grass is similar to the Bluegrasses in shape, that is, the panicle is open and feathery; however, the two species are unrelated, as Hair Grass belongs to the Timothy Tribe, characterized by having only one floret per spikelet. The florets are very tiny in this tribe and it takes some patience to squeeze out the single fruit (seed). Large panicles of Hair Grass often break off in autumn and roll along the ground like miniature tumbleweeds.

The specific name *"scabra"* means "rough". Rub your fingers along the grass blades to feel the distinct sandpaper effect.

Hair Grass is found on moist prairie and readily invades open, disturbed areas. Look for it near the gravel pit.

Blue Grama
Bouteloua gracilis

Blue Grama is a graceful (hence its specific name, *gracilis*), densely tufted, low (20-30 cm) perennial which is the dominant species on the drier Mixed Grass Ecoregion east of Calgary.

Blue Grama may not be readily noticed among the taller prairie grasses, but once found and identified it is easy to remember. With its equal length spikelets forming "comblike" on the upward side of the bent stem, the inflorescence resembles a blueish upturned brush. The leaf blades are narrow and often curled. No other grass on Nose Hill has the comblike inflorescence.

Blue Grama Grass (Bouteloua gracilis)   *Spear Grass (Stipa comata)*

On Nose Hill, Blue Grama can be found on dry, south-facing slopes often in association with Needle-and-Thread Grass. The hill alongside the path leading from 14th Street has stands of Blue Grama from approximately half-way up.

Blue Grama provides excellent forage for wild and domestic animals. Bison favour this species and another common name is Buffalo Grass. It belongs to the Grama Tribe (Chlorideae).

Spear Grass or Needle-and-Thread   *Stipa comata*

Needle-and-Thread Grass is a common, robust prairie grass on dry sites. It is a bunchgrass (and therefore does not have rhizomes but relies on seed propagation), with narrow (2 mm wide) leaf blades.

The panicle is long and loosely narrow with many spikelets each with one floret. A distinctive characteristic of Needle-and-Thread is the extremely long awn (to 10 cm long) which extends from the floret. The awns are slightly twisted and when the floret (seed) is ready to fall (disarticulate) the awns twist and aid in "springing" it and its accompanying awn from the plant. The florets are sharp with backward-pointed barbs which, like fish-hooks, are easy to insert and difficult to remove.

A walk along the south-facing slopes of Nose Hill in the fall often results in a good collection of Needle-and-Thread florets in one's clothing.

Needle-and-Thread belongs to the Timothy Tribe (Agrostideae) along with the commonly-known Timothy Grass (not described). A major characteristic of this tribe is a single floret in the spikelet.

Further Reading

Best, Keith F., Jan Looman and J. Baden Campbell 1971 *Prairie Grasses*. Publication 1413. Canada Department of Agriculture. Information Canada, Ottawa, Ontario
Moss, E.H. 1959 *Flora of Alberta*.
Packer, John G. 1983 *Flora of Alberta*. Revised Second Edition. University of Toronto Press, Toronto, Ontario

Mushrooms of Nose Hill   R.M. Danielson

The fungal flora of Nose Hill is no doubt richer than is indicated by collections made up to the present time. Less than three dozen species of fungi that produce large or conspicuous fruit bodies (mushrooms) have been recorded from this part of Calgary and on most days no fleshy fungi can be found even with intense searching. This is not due to the absence of these fungi, but rather, due to the generally adverse conditions for fruiting that occur on Nose Hill. The major limiting factor for the development of the mycelium (the threads that form the vegetative phase of the fungus) and the fruitbody (the sexual reproductive structure) is water.

The grassland landscape normally receives only brief episodes of precipitation during the growing season and the surface soils are quickly dried by the wind which sweeps over the hill. Even in the winter, the soils are dry and snow can only accumulate in substantial quantities in the sheltered ravines, thus reducing the springtime pulse of saturating water at the time of snowmelt. As a result of these two climatic factors, low precipitation and wind, fruiting of fungi is a relatively rare occurrence, and those fungi that do fruit show adaptations to overcoming or taking advantage of these conditions.

The mushrooms of greatest interest on Nose Hill are those of the true grassland portions of the hill, as they are limited in distribution to this habitat and illustrate adaptations to this stressed environment. The group most likely to be encountered on the exposed areas of the hill are Puffballs. The Puffballs are characterized by producing a more-or-less round, tough sac in which the sexual spores reach maturity protected from the desiccating forces of low humidity and wind. Once the spores are mature the Puffballs demonstrate a variety of methods to disseminate their spores efficiently. The function of the spores is, like those of all the other fungi, to disperse the species to new habitats and to establish new centres of vegetative activity. A single Puffball may produce billions of spores but only a very minute fraction of these will land on a suitable habitat and encounter favourable conditions for growth. The vast majority of spores perish in their attempt to proliferate the species.

Perhaps the most simply adapted Puffball to windswept Nose Hill is *Bovista plumbea*. This species is also known as "the tumbler", a name reflecting its method of spore dissemination. Fruitbodies of *Bovista* are simple spheres that mature on the soil surface. When mature the fruit-bodies break loose from the soil and the wind blows the 1-3 cm diameter spheres over the landscape. As they are blown about, the outer wall layer is eroded exposing the bluish or purplish grey, paper-thin, inner wall which has a single, rough opening. With the tumbling about, spores spill out of the opening onto the soil — a clear adaptation to open, windy environments.

The largest mush-rooms that occur on Nose Hill are two species of *Calvatia,* the genus that con-tains the Giant Puff-ball, which may be up to 60 cm in diameter. *Calvatia bovista* and *Calvatia cyathiformis* are smaller, 10-15 cm in diameter, and are pure white when

Puffball (Calvatia cyathiformis)

young. As they mature, the outer wall of the spore sac darkens and begins to crack. Both of these large Puffballs have thick bases which remain firmly attached to the prairie soil; so firmly in fact that the bases may remain in place for a year or more. Unlike some other Puffballs found on Nose Hill in which the spore sac has a definite opening at the top, species of *Calvatia* require weathering and wind to free the spores. The action of the wind slowly erodes away the protective spore sac wall until the spore mass is exposed, and only then can the spores be dispersed.

Puffballs of Nose Hill that develop distinct apical openings of the spore sac include species of *Lycoperdon, Geastrum* and *Tulostoma. Lycoper-don polymorphum* and *Lycoperdon umbrinum,* the latter found in wooded ravines, produce small roundish fruitbodies with a flexible-walled spore sac and a small apical pore. The spore sacs in these species act somewhat like a bellows and the spores are expelled through the pore in little "puffs", as either the wind buffets the dry fruitbodies, or the wall is struck by falling raindrops or wind-driven debris.

A somewhat more sophisticated Puffball is *Geastrum floriformes,* a member of the Earthstar group. This small Puffball develops partially buried in the soil, where it is protected from the ever-present drying wind. At first the fruitbody is spherical, but as it matures the outer layer of the wall splits radially from the top downward, like pieces of orange peel, and assumes a star-like pattern. As the wall continues to dry and the spores mature in the central spore sac, the rays of the outer wall recurve downward until the rays actually lift the spore sac into the turbulent air. In this elevated position the spores are dispersed as they are in *Lycoperdon*.

The last species of Puffball to be recorded from Nose Hill (but surely not the last to occur there) is *Tulostoma simulans*. This is one of the stalked Puffballs in which a little spore sac, about 1 cm in diameter with a single apical pore, is positioned on top of a slender, tough stalk about 2 cm in height. The stalk ensures that the spore sac, which is filled with a fine brown powder of spores, is in an optimal position for the wind to carry the spores to new locations.

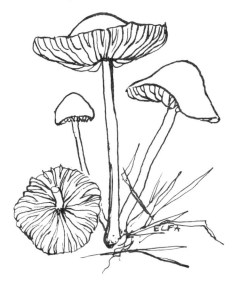

Fairy Ring Mushroom (Marasmius oreades)

The Puffball way-of-life is only one of the adaptations to windy, dry conditions that can be found among the Nose Hill fungi. Another adaptation to the fleeting soil moisture can be found with the common Fairy Ring Mushroom, *Marasmius oreades*. The Fairy Ring Mushroom fits the typical description of an agaric mushroom with a cap, gills on which the spores are borne, and a central stem. Most mushrooms are subject to desiccation, and if dry conditions occur during development, the mushrooms are doomed. The Fairy Ring Mushroom, however, has resolved this intermittent moisture problem within the structure of its fruitbody. When drying conditions occur, the fruitbody of *Marasmius oreades* does indeed dry up, but the process is reversible and when rainfall returns the shrivelled mushrooms revive and immediately begin producing spores. This cycle of drying and reviving can be repeated several times due to the very tough nature of the mycelium from which the mushroom is constructed. This process serves to increase the efficiency of the fungus as the same fruitbody remains functional for a long period of time, and entirely new mushrooms need not be produced for each successive period of favourable moisture conditions.

The common name, Fairy Ring Mushroom, arose from the habit of fruiting in distinct circles or rings. These rings originate from a spore landing on the soil, germinating, and the mycelium growing out at the same rate in all directions. The mycelium may grow at a rate of about 30 cm per year and thus the ring enlarges every year. When conditions (moisture, temperature) are right, the mycelium will produce mushrooms at the outer margin of the ring resulting in circles of mushrooms in the grass. Many other species may produce fruitbodies in rings and some of these may be noticed in the absence of fruitbodies as the mycelium can kill the vegetation while others may enhance the growth of grasses. In the case of *Marasmius oreades,* the vegetation is injured as the mycelium makes the soil of the outer ring nonwettable and droughty, while conversely, the decomposing activity of the mycelium releases nitrogen, a mineral nutrient which produces a lush ring of dark green grass on the inside of the fruitbody ring.

Another fungus which may form fairy rings is *Agaricus campestris,* the Meadow Mushroom. It occurs on Nose Hill along with at least one other species of Agaricus but fairy rings have not been observed there. *Agaricus campestris* is one of the most common grassland fungi and forms large, robust mushrooms. It is subject to intermittent drying and dead, half-developed mushrooms that were caught by droughty conditions are not an uncommon sight. Adaptations that appear to reduce the chances for aborted development are the protective veil that covers the developing gills and the short, stout stature of the mushroom. Species of *Agaricus* that fruit in forests have long, slender stems, whereas those found in grasslands, where moisture conditions are more erratic, have short, stout stems. This stature adaptation is also demonstrated by the occurrence of *Clitocybe praemagna* on Nose Hill. This species is known from only a few other locations in North America, all prairie habitats. The fruitbody of *Clitocybe praemagna* has a very stout stature, whereas most other *Clitocybes* are slender and occur in woodlands.

In addition to the grassland fungi, several other ecological groups of mushrooms occur on Nose Hill. One of these is the dung fungus which fruits on the droppings of grazing mammals. In the past they may have occurred on buffalo dung but currently they can be found on horse dung. The two species found so far are *Panaeolus separatus* and *Stropharia semiglobata.* Both of these species are adapted to rapidly producing relatively delicate fruitbodies on a substrate that can quickly dry out. The dung is nutrient-rich and could support the growth of many mushrooms, but as with the mushrooms found on the soil, the limiting factor for fungal growth is moisture. Thus the quick-maturing, short-lived species are favoured and they produce pulses of small mushrooms in response to rainshowers.

When one moves from the grassland to the wooded ravines of Nose Hill, two additional groups of fungi may be encountered: the wood-decay fungi and the mycorrhizal fungi. The wood-decay fungi are

Schizophyllum commune:
a bracket fungus

similar to those found in other areas in the Calgary region and do not demonstrate any special adaptations to the transitional nature of their Nose Hill habitat. Small bracket fungi are common on the logs of Aspen and include *Trichaptum biformis* with its violet-coloured pore layer, *Bjerkandera adusta* with smoky pores, *Schizophyllum commune* with split gills, and several more species. On standing Aspen the hoof-shaped conks of *Phellinus tremulae* are indicators of the certain demise of individual trees due to heart-rot and subsequent windthrow. Dead branches of Aspen may be covered with hundreds of coral spots of *Nectria cinnabarina* or the reddish wart-like fruitbodies of *Peniophora rufa*. Of interest on rotting Aspen logs are two colourful cup fungi, *Bisporella citrina* and *Chlorociboria aeruginascens*. The former produces multitudes of tiny, yellow disc-like fruitbodies whereas the latter's fruitbodies are blue-green and stain the decaying wood the same colour.

Few mycorrhizal fungi have been reported from Nose Hill but many species certainly occur in association with the Aspen and Willows. These fungi form obligate symbiotic relationships with the roots of specific host plants and, to date, only a few individuals of *Inocybe* and *Cortinarius* have been seen.

In summary, many interesting mushrooms have been observed on Nose Hill and many more await discovery. They form an essential part of the grassland community and a study of their ecology and morphology reveals the current status of the evolution of forms to an environment that experiences great stresses in moisture, soil nutrients, and exposure to insolation and wind.

Further Reading

Arora, D. 1986 *Mushrooms Demystified.* Ten Speed Press, Berkeley, California

Lincoff, G.H. 1981 *The Audubon Society Field Guide to North American Mushrooms.* Alfred Knopf, Inc., New York, New York.

McKenny, M., D.E. Stuntz and J.F. Ammirati 1987 *The New Savory Wild Mushroom.* Western Producer Prairie Books, Saskatoon, Sask.

Miller, O.K., Jr. 1971 *Mushrooms of North America.* E.P. Dutton, New York, New York

Lichens

Maxwell Capen

Introduction

Lichens are non-vascu-
lar, ie. have no woody
tissue. They are plants
that consist mainly of
two components, one of
which is a green or blue-
green alga and the other
of colourless fungal
threads (hyphae). Both
live together in a har-

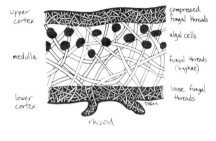

Section through a Lichen

moniously-balanced life-form called symbiosis. The alga produces food
by photo-synthesis, and the fungus lives off this nourishment. It
generally makes up the greater portion of the plant. The fungal threads
absorb moisture.

There are three main types of lichens that are distinguished by growth
form, and by the manner in which they are attached to the material on
which they grow (substratum). There are many intermediate forms between these types. In addition, colour may, in many instances, be a
distinctive factor.

Crustose lichens are crust-like in form, closely attached to the substratum, and are very difficult, if not impossible, to separate from it.

Foliose lichens have a flattened or prostrate form and growth is horizontal; they have a leafy or scale-like appearance. Generally these
lichens are loosely attached to the substratum.

Fruticose lichens have lichen bodies generally round in cross-section but
some are somewhat flattened. They can be erect or pendent; some of
these are bushy or hair-like in appearance. Common features of some
of these are their cup-like shape. These "cups" grow at the end of
upright stems (podetia).

Because lichens are able to absorb dissolved substances from the atmo-
sphere, they are very sensitive to pollution and are therefore good

indicators of sulphur dioxide contamination.

It is interesting to note that Latin names are used almost exclusively for these plants, and only comparatively few lichens have English common names. For example "Dog Lichen", *Peltigera canina,* is one which is commonly observed, and was named during medieval times because of its use in the treatment of rabies. Another is called "Tree Lungwort", *Lobaria pulmonaria,* because of its resemblance to lung tissue, and was used during the same period for the treatment of diseases of the chest. This is an example of the "Doctrine of Signatures"; that is, plants which resemble parts of the body were used to cure those parts when diseased.

Lichens of Nose Hill

Some of the more common species of lichens observed in the Nose Hill area are listed below. For simplicity, these are described briefly. The descriptions are mainly based on their colour, which can change when wet, and the type of lichen (ie. growth-form), and the kind of material to which they are attached.

Rocks

Xanthoria elegans (Teloschistaceae)
It is bright orange in colour and is mostly found on rocks (crustose).

Dimelaena oreina (Physciaceae)
This lichen is yellow or yellowish-grey and can be seen on quartzite erratics (crustose), for example, on the Buffalo rubbing-stones.

Leconora muralis (Lecanoraceae)
Generally green to whitish yellow, and is found on sandstone (crustose).

Leconora alphoplaca (Lecanoraceae)
It is generally found on sandstone and is mainly whitish-grey (crustose).

Trees

Candelaria concolor (Parmeliaceae)
The colour is bright yellow or yellowish-lemon, and it has spots on its surface called soredia. It is found on Willow branches (crustose).

Parmelia exasperatula (Parmeliaceae)
It has a dark olive-brown colour, and can be observed on Willow branches (foliose).

Usnea compacta (Usneaceae)
The colour is bright green to straw-yellow, and some forms have a cushion-like appearance. It is found on Willow branches (fruticose).

Xanthoria polycarpa (Teloschistaceae)
Nearly always bright orange in colour. It is seen on branches and trunks of Willow and Aspen trees (foliose).

Soil

Cladonia pyxidata (Cladoniaceae)
Primarily greenish-mineral-grey. This lichen is found occasionally on the soil, and has deep cups on the apices of its stems (podetia); (fruticose).

Lecidea decipiens (Lecideaceae)
It is dark orange and is found on exposed ridges (fruticose).

Peltigera rufescens (Peltigeraceae)
When dry this lichen is light greyish-green but is dark green when wet. Sometimes it is called "Studded Leather Lichen" because of numerous very small bump-like growths on its surface. These are called cephalodia (foliose).

Further Reading

Hale, Mason E. 1969 *The Lichens.* W.M.C. Brown, Publishers, Dubuque, Iowa
Alvin, Kenneth 1977 *The Observer's Book of Lichens.* F. Warner Ltd., London, England

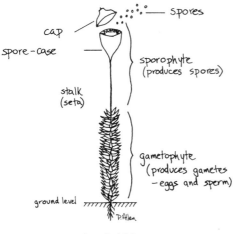

Mosses

Maxwell Capen

Introduction

Mosses are plants that lack any true woody tissue, that is, they are non-vascular. They are attached to the ground by rhizoids, which are not true roots.

A typical Moss

There are two principal types of growth. They may have stalks rising erect from the end of the leafy stem, with capsules growing from their tips and possessing only a few branches, or they may have many lateral prostrate branches, which form mats, with their capsules on stalks arising along their stems.

Like lichens, they do not have many common English names. However, there are a few, such as the "Hair Cap" mosses, which include all species of *Polytrichum* and *Pogonatum,* and the "Feather" mosses which include among others *Ptilium, Hylocomium* and *Pleurozium.*

There are some plants that resemble mosses but are not mosses, a few of which are the "Club-mosses", which have a vascular system, "Reindeer Mosses", which are lichens, and "Spanish Mosses", which are flowering plants, belonging to the Pineapple family.

Some mosses can grow on exposed rock surfaces and tolerate drying-out periods, but most species found in the Nose Hill area are found in the ravines, mostly on the north-facing slopes, and in Aspen groves.

They are all soil pioneers, producing a chemical breakdown of the rock surface, forming soil suitable for colonization by various vascular plants.

Mosses of Nose Hill

The mosses that are more commonly observed in the Nose Hill area are described below, with the majority found in ravines where there are Aspen groves, or bushes. One rare moss, *Weissia controversa,* found on Nose Hill, is of special interest because it has been observed in only one other place in Alberta.

Hypnum cupressiforme (Hypnaceae)
This moss is seen occasionally on soil associated with Aspen groves.

Orthotrichum obtusifolium (Orthotrichaceae)
Occasionally observed on Willow scrub.

Pylaisiella (Pylaisia) polyantha (Hypnaceae)
This is a common moss which occurs in dense mats in a "stocking-like" form at the base of Aspen trees, around the trunk.

Tortula ruralis (Pottiaceae)
A common moss seen on soil, associated with Aspen groves.

Further Reading

Conrad, H.S. 1956 *The Mosses and Liverworts.* Revised Edition. W.M.C. Brown, Publishers, Dubuque, Iowa

Skippers and Butterflies   Harold Pinel

Introduction

Butterflies are insects, therefore, like all insects, have 6 jointed legs, 3 body segments and 2 antennae. Along with the more numerous moths, butterflies make up the Order Lepidoptera, whose members differ from all other insects in having scales over all or most of their wings, and often on the body as well. Within the Lepidoptera, butterflies and moths are separated from each other by their body structure, wing venation and habits. Butterflies fly during the day; most moths are nocturnal. Butterflies at rest tend to hold the wings vertically over the back, while moths may either fold the wings tentlike over the back, wrap them around the body, or extend them to the sides. Butterflies have knoblike clubs at the tips of the antennae; moths lack antennal clubs.

Like most other insects a butterfly passes through four very different stages in the course of its life: egg, larva, pupa and adult. After mating, female butterflies lay eggs either singly, or in rows, chains, or clusters, of a few to several hundred eggs. The egg shape and texture vary greatly among species. Some eggs don't hatch until the following spring, while others hatch before winter.

The larva, or caterpillar, has simple eyes, chewing jaws and 3 pairs of jointed legs near the front as well as 5 pairs of grasping prolegs near the rear. The caterpillar spends its life feeding; the more it eats, the larger it grows. However, because its skin cannot stretch, the caterpillar grows by molting its skin several times — each stage, called an instar, is larger than the previous one. The final molt produce the pupa or chrysalis.

The pupa is a resting stage and does not feed. The pupae of most butterflies are naked, unlike those of moths, which are protected by a silken cocoon. The pupae of many butterflies hang by the tail end; others hang upright, supported by a silken girdle. Some pupae are green or brown, resembling leaves, stems, or wood. Others are brightly variegated and covered with thorny bumps.

When the adult is fully formed, the chrysalis skin splits open, permitting the butterfly to crawl out. It soon begins to pump fluids from its swollen body into its shrunken wings. As soon as the adult can fly, courtship begins, sometimes involving elaborate dances, prenuptial flights, or mutual wing strokings. Mating usually lasts several hours. The adult's lifespan ranges from a week to 6 to 8 months, depending upon the species, with most averaging 2 weeks.

Distribution

A combination of many factors affects the distribution of butterflies — the plants they eat, their tolerance of moisture and temperature, their ability to reach new areas, and changes in the landscape. Both the caterpillars and adult butterflies require specific kinds of plants and habitats. For this reason, butterflies are especially vulnerable to land development. Widespread use of pesticides further reduces butterfly populations. Many North American species are declining in range and in numbers. Prairie grasslands, wetlands such as bogs and marshes, sand dunes and virgin forests are among the most imperiled butterfly habitats. Butterflies are significant plant pollinators as well as indicators of ecological quality in our environment.

To date, more butterfly species have been recorded for Nose Hill than for any other natural area in Calgary. There is, however, still much to learn about the butterflies of Nose Hill. For example, more information is needed on species abundance, population trends, flight periods, and effects of peripheral land development. Most of the butterfly species are residents, but there are a few irregular migrants and windblown strays. The best times to observe butterflies on Nose Hill are bright sunny days from April to September. During this 6-month period, there are major differences in the quantity and diversity of the butterflies.

April to Mid-May

The Mourning Cloak butterfly which is dark purple-brown with yellow or white wing margins, overwinters as an adult, and is one of the first butterflies to be seen in the spring. Another group of butterflies which hibernate as adults are the Anglewings, genus *Polygonia*. After mating, Mourning Cloaks and Anglewings lay their eggs on the buds of Willows, Poplars, Nettles and Gooseberries which they use as food plants. Other butterflies to be seen at this time of year on Nose Hill include the Alberta Arctic, Western White, Cabbage White, Milbert's Tortoiseshell and Red-disked Alpine.

Mid-May to July

Many of the spring butterfly species found on Nose Hill are still present during this time period, but their wings have often become dull and worn. Some species have been succeeded by new arrivals, including a number of Blues and Satyrs.

The Blues are small butterflies, most of which have metallic blue scaling on their wings. They feed largely on plants of the legume family. Each species of Blue in Alberta has a distinctive underwing pattern. Common Blues on Nose Hill include the Silvery Blue, Melissa Blue, Greenish Blue and Arctic Blue.

The Satyrs of this season are small or medium-sized brown butterflies. The niche occupied by the Alberta Arctic in early spring is now filled by the Prairie Ringlet and Common Alpine.

The Fritillaries, a group of butterflies whose wings are characterized by black markings on an orange background, make their appearance. The more common Fritillaries include the Callippe Fritillary, Atlantis Fritillary and Mormon Fritillary.

Many skippers also make their first appearance at this time. Two species that are commonly encountered include the Persius Duskywing and the Garita Skipperling.

Common Sulphurs are commonly observed flying in all habitats on the hill, and Tiger Swallowtails are occasionally seen in the wooded coulees.

July to September

The change from season to season is gradual but fewer butterfly species are in evidence. The majority of those seen will be Sulphurs and Fritillaries. The most common Satyr at this time is now the Large Wood Nymph. During late July and August, the Melissa Blue is the only Blue still flying. Mourning Cloaks appear in late August for a few weeks before going into hibernation, from which they may reappear during the fall on the occasional warm sunny day.

Annotated List

A total of 49 species of skippers and butterflies have been recorded for Nose Hill. They are listed below in the taxonomic order and nomenclature as outlined by Miller and Brown (1981). Common names are from Pyle (1981).

Besides the author, many of the species listed below were recorded by Peter Allen, Robert L. Anderson and Charles Bird. Books that may be used for identifying the butterflies include Hooper (1973), Howe (1975), and Pyle (1981).

Family Hesperiidae

Dreamy Duskywing   *Erynnis icelus*
Uncommon in the wooded coulees from mid-May to mid-June.

Persius Duskywing   *Erynnis persius*
Common in the grasslands and shrub communities. It has been recorded from May 25 to June 28.

Two-banded Checkered Skipper   *Pyrgus ruralis*
Rare in the grasslands. A male was collected on May 26, 1956. It probably only occurs in the area as a rare wind-blown stray.

Common Checkered Skipper   *Pyrgus communis*
Occasional in the grasslands from early June to mid-August.

Arctic Skipper   *Carterocephalus palaemon*
Rare, a male was collected on May 29, 1957.

Garita Skipperling   *Oarisma garita*
Fairly common in the grasslands. The recorded flight period is from June 20 to July 18.

Common Branded Skipper   *Hesperia comma assiniboia*
Uncommon in grasslands where the flight period has been recorded from June 4 to September 19.

Yellowpatch Skipper   *Polites coras*
Fairly common in grasslands and disturbed areas from late June to early August.

Draco Skipper   *Polites draco*
Individuals have been recorded in the grasslands during June.

Tawny-edged Skipper   *Polites themistocles*
Occasional in native and disturbed grasslands. The flight period has been recorded from June 22 to July 19.

Long Dash   *Polites mystic dacotah*
Scarce in the grasslands in late June and early July.

Family Papilionidae

Anise Swallowtail   *Papilio zelicaon nitra*
Occasional in grasslands. It flies during June.

Western White (Pontia occidentalis)
(on Wild Mustard)

Tiger Swallowtail
Pterourus glaucus
canadensis
Uncommon in Aspen woods and shrub communities. The flight period has been recorded from June 4 to June 26.

Family Pieridae

Western White
Pontia occidentalis
Common in grasslands and disturbed areas. The flight period has been recorded from April 21 to September 17.

Cabbage White   *Artogeia rapae*
Fairly common in disturbed areas and grasslands from May to early August.

Common Sulphur (Colias philodice eriphyle)
(on Alfalfa flowers)

Common Sulphur
Colias philodice eriphyle
Common in all habitats on Nose Hill. Its recorded flight period is from May 17 to September 6. Albinistic females are not uncommon.

Queen Alexandra's Sulphur
Colias alexandra astraea
Fairly common in grasslands and shrub communities. The recorded flight period is June 24 to August 25.

Family Lycaenidae

Purplish Copper
Epidemia helloides
Scarce in the damp areas

in the ravines where it has been recorded only from August 19 to September 6.

Coral Hairstreak *Harkenclenus titus immaculosus*
Occasional in the shrub communities. The recorded flight period is June 29 to August 23.

Brown Elfin *Incisalia augustus*
Rare; two individuals were collected on south-facing grassland slopes May 11, 1973.

Hoary Elfin *Incisalia polios obscurus*
Rare, an individual was collected in a shrub community on May 11, 1973.

Western Tailed Blue *Everes amyntula albrighti*
Scarce, near Aspen groves in June.

Silvery Blue *Glaucopsyche lygdamus couperi*
Common in the grasslands. Flight period has been recorded from May 10 to July 13.

Melissa Blue
Lycaeides melissa
Common in the grasslands, with a recorded flight period of June 5 to August 23.

Greenish Blue
Plebejus saepiolus amica
Common in grasslands. The flight period has been recorded from June 5 to July 20.

Common Blue
Icaricia icarioides pembina
Scarce in late June in the grasslands.

Melissa Blue (Lycaeides melissa)

Acmon Blue *Icaricia acmon lutzi*
Rare on south-facing grassland slopes.

Arctic Blue *Agriades franklinii rustica*
Common in the grasslands where it has been recorded flying from June 3 to July 6.

Family Nymphalidae

Great Spangled Fritillary *Speyeria cybele pseudocarpenteri*
Uncommon in shrub communities. The flight period is July 9 to August 15.

Aphrodite   *Speyeria aphrodite*
Uncommon in grasslands from July 27 to August 23.

Callippe Fritillary   *Speyeria callippe calgariana*
Uncommon in grasslands. The recorded flight period is from June 19 to
July 26.

Atlantis Fritillary   *Speyeria atlantis beani*
Common in grasslands and shrub communities, where the flight period
has been recorded from June 7 to July 24.

Mormon Fritillary
(Speyeria mormonia)

Mormon Fritillary
Speyeria mormonia
Fairly common in grasslands
and shrub communities. The
flight period has been recorded
from June 3 to August 14.

Meadow Fritillary
Clossiana bellona jenistae
Fairly common in grasslands
and shrub communities. It has
only been recorded flying from
May 16 to June 4.

Gorgone Crescentspot
Charidryas gorgone carlota
A male was collected on June 5,
1957. This species has since
probably vanished from Nose
Hill.

Pearly Crescentspot
Phyciodes tharos
An individual was collected in a
shrub community on July 7,
1973.

Field Crescentspot   *Phyciodes pratensis*
Rare in shrub communities. This species is at the eastern edge of its
known range in Alberta on Nose Hill, so its normal occurrence here is
doubtful.

Gray Comma   *Polygonia progne*
One female was collected in Aspen woods on August 3, 1959.

Mourning Cloak   *Nymphalis antiopa antiopa*
Fairly common in Aspen woods and shrub communities. The flight
periods are April 21 to May 24, and August 19 to September 19.

Milbert's Tortoiseshell *Aglais milberti furcillata*
Common in Aspen woods, shrub communities and disturbed grasslands. The flight period has been recorded from April 21 to August 31.

Painted Lady *Vanessa cardui*
This species is an irregular migrant from the United States. Good numbers were observed in 1973 and 1983. It has been observed flying from mid-May until the end of September. It is not associated with any particular habitat.

Red Admiral *Vanessa atalanta rubria*
Scarce in disturbed grasslands. It has been recorded in June and August.

White Admiral *Basilarchia arthemis rubrofasciata*
Fairly common in Aspen woods and shrub communities from June 1 to July 7.

Family Satyridae

Prairie Ringlet
Coenonympha inornata benjamini
Fairly common in grasslands. The flight period has been recorded from June 3 to July 20.

Large Wood Nymph
Cercyonis pegala ino
Common in grasslands, where it has been recorded flying from June 3 to July 30.

Red-disked Alpine
Erebia discoidalis mcdunnoughi
Uncommon in grasslands.

Large Wood Nymph on Tufted Fleabane
(Cercyonis pegala ino)

On Nose Hill, it has only been recorded during May, to date.

Common Alpine *Erebia epipsodea*
Fairly common in grasslands from May 29 to July 9.

Uhler's Arctic *Oeneis uhleri varuna*
Fairly common in grasslands. The flight period has been recorded from May 25 to June 23.

Alberta Arctic *Oeneis alberta*
Fairly common in grasslands during the first three weeks of May.

Further Reading

Hooper, R.R. 1973 *Butterflies of Saskatchewan.* Saskatchewan Department of Natural Resources. Museum of Natural History, Regina, Saskatchewan

Howe, W.H. 1975 *The Butterflies of North America.* Doubleday & Company Inc., New York, New York

Miller, L.D. and F.M. Brown 1981 *A Catalogue/Checklist of the Butterflies of America North of Mexico.* The Lepidopterists' Society. Memoir No. 2, Sarasota, Florida

Pinel, H.W. (Ed.) 1981 *Calgary's Natural Areas.* Calgary Field Naturalists' Society

Pyle, R.M. 1981 *The Audubon Society Field Guide to North American Butterflies.* Chanticleer Press Inc., New York, New York.

Birds   Don Stiles

How Birds are Adapted for Flight

The wings of a bird are modifications of the front legs (or arms). The two bones of the forearm, the radius and ulna, are still distinct, but the carpal bones (the wrist), the meta-carpals (the hand) and the phalanges (the fingers) have been more or less fused together into a firm base. The primary feathers are attached to this base, and the secondary feathers are attached to the ulna of the forearm. A group of feathers called the "alula" is borne by the "thumb".

Feathers (unique to birds) have evolved from reptilian scales, and have a delicate and complicated structure. The interlocking barbs and barbules give lightness and strength and are perfectly adapted to aid the bird in flight.

The breast muscles of birds are very strong and highly developed in order to move the wings. These pectoral muscles are attached to the breast bone, which has developed a well-marked "keel" — a characteristic feature of bird skeletons. Many of the birds' bones are hollow and this makes the skeleton lighter.

Reference

Tyne, Josselyn & Andrew J. Berger 1971 *Fundamentals of Ornithology.* Dover Publications Inc., New York, New York.

Nose Hill Birds

Over the years naturalists have recorded approximately 100 species of birds on Nose Hill. Many of these are occasional migrants or visitors. This compilation describes only the 53 most common species of birds seen. They are divided up into the following groups:

Residents can be found year round.

Winter Visitors appear only in the winter, having spent the remainder of the year farther north.

Migrants come through in the spring on their way north, spend their summer farther north, and return south in the fall.

Summer Residents come to Nose Hill to nest and raise their young.

Visitors reside in the Calgary area, and visit or fly over Nose Hill fairly often but do not nest there.

Descriptions of the common field marks and habitats are provided so that even the novice can know what to look for. Following the descriptions are the dates when to expect each of the species on Nose Hill. For a better knowledge of how to identify birds, a field guide such as "Birds of North America" by Robbins et al is recommended. Further confidence in bird identification can be obtained by taking a city-sponsored birdwatching course at the Inglewood Bird Sanctuary.

Residents

Sharp-tailed Grouse
Nose Hill is one of the few places within Calgary City limits where this species is found. They are fairly elusive, but are usually found on the Calgary Christmas Bird Count. Their best identifying field-mark is the white-edged sharp tail seen best when flying away. Nesting is probable.

Ring-necked Pheasant
The male of this introduced species is colourful, with a reddish patch on the side of the face, and a long tail. The female is a drab brown but can still be identified by the long tail. Ring-necked Pheasants may nest on Nose Hill but this is uncertain.

Gray Partridge*
Usually found in the grasslands in the summer and thickets in the winter. You may expect to flush up flocks of 5 to 20 most of the year, but usually only pairs during the breeding season in May. Young may be seen in June or July.

* Known to nest on Nose Hill.

Sharp-tailed Grouse   *Ring-necked Pheasant*

Gray Partridge

Great Horned Owl

Great Horned Owl*
This large owl is our most common owl in the Calgary area. Although not seen on a regular basis, it may sometimes be spotted sitting in the thickest Aspen groves.

Downy Woodpecker
Our smallest woodpecker, a year-round black and white woodpecker occasionally found in Poplar groves. The red patch on the back of the male's head can sometimes be seen. Nesting has not been confirmed.

Black-billed Magpie*
This long-tailed black and white scavenger is the bird you are most likely to see year round.

Downy Woodpecker

Black-billed Magpie

Black-capped Chickadee

This small black-capped bird with a large white patch below the eyes and a long tail is one of the most common small birds you are likely to see, especially in the Aspens in the winter. Nesting is probable.

European Starling*

An introduced bird which has become common. They can be seen most of the year except in the coldest winter months when they look for warmer parts of Calgary. Many Starlings migrate to warmer climates, but a few always stay through the winter.

Winter Visitors

Bohemian Waxwing

Many Calgary residents are familiar with the flocks of these crested birds which come to feed on their Mountain Ash or Crabapple trees. They can be distinguished from the summer residents, the Cedar Waxwings, because the Bohemian Waxwing has white patches on the wing and cinnamon under the tail while the Cedar Waxwing does not. Mid-October to April.

Common Redpoll

These small birds usually come into Calgary in the winter to feed on weed seeds. They are red-capped, and the male has a reddish patch on his chest and rump also. In some winters, they are absent from Nose Hill. Sometimes, within flocks of Common Redpolls, you may find paler birds with a white rump patch. These are another species, the Hoary Redpoll.
Mid-October to mid-April.

Snow Bunting

Snow Bunting

These primarily white birds can usually be found in flocks on Nose Hill prairies in winter. In some years they are not present, or are seen only in small numbers.
Mid-October to mid-April.

Bohemian Waxwing   *Black-capped Chickadee*

Migrants

Mallard

Flocks of Mallards are sometimes seen flying over Nose Hill. Usually these are migrating, but in 1986 a Mallard nest was found on Nose Hill.

Rough-legged Hawk

This Hawk is an early and late migrant en route to and from the Arctic where it breeds. Expect to see them in the early spring, and in late fall. Their predominant markings are dark "wrist" marks on the under side of the wings.

North movement: Late March to mid-April.
South movement: Mid-October.
An occasional bird may overwinter.

Water Pipit

These birds look like sparrows, but have a thinner bill. Field marks are a streaked, buffy breast and white tail flanks. They always travel in flocks.

North movement: mid-April.
South movement: first half of October.

Yellow-rumped Warbler

This is by far the most common Warbler. In the spring their markings — white on the throat, yellow under the wing and on the rump — are easily identified. In the fall, the young birds are the most numerous and often few markings are in evidence. Sometimes one of the above markings such as the yellow rump patch may be seen, but often the observer sees only a small beige bird with a white eye ring and white wing bars, and some beige streaking just below the wings.

North movement: late April through May.
South movement: late August to early October.

Dark-eyed Junco

This gray bird with a white belly and white outer tail feathers can sometimes be found migrating through, usually in flocks.

North movement: first half of April.
South movement: mid-September.

Tree Sparrow

These are also early and late migrants as they fly to the Arctic. They are fairly shy birds so they are hard to identify. However, if you see a flock of sparrows in April or October and you spot at least one of these features — a central breast spot, white wing bars, or a rusty cap — they are most likely Tree Sparrows.

North movement: mid-March to mid-April.
South movement: mid-September to late October.
They are present through some winters in small numbers.

White-crowned Sparrow

The name identifies these sparrows in the spring. In the fall they are harder to identify as you will see mostly young birds and their crown is buffy instead of white.

North movement: late April to early May.
South movement: mid-September to early October.

White-throated Sparrow

The name also identifies this Sparrow. They also have a distinctive song which could be translated as "Oh sweet Canada, Canada", and is easily recognized even if you don't see the bird.

North movement: late April to early May.
South movement: mid-September to mid-October.

Both the White-crowned and White-throated Sparrow have unstreaked breasts. They are both partial to wooded areas rather than grasslands.

Tree Sparrow

White-crowned Sparrow

Red-tailed Hawk

Northern Harrier

Summer Residents and Visitors

(All are summer residents unless noted.)

Red-tailed Hawk*
One of the common large summer hawks of the Calgary area. Usually it can be identified by its red tail. In some individuals where the tail is paler, the next best field mark is a darker band across the centre of otherwise white underparts.
Late March or early April to first half of October.

Swainson's Hawk*
The common large hawk of the prairies, often seen soaring over Nose Hill. Easily identified from below due to the dark front part of the breast, and white on the front part of the wings and dark on the back part. Occasionally, a dark-phase individual is seen where the contrast in the wings between the lighter front and the darker back is hard to

Swainson's Hawk

Killdeer

distinguish. Swainson's Hawks soar with a slight V, whereas the Red-tailed Hawk soars with its wings flat — another field mark if you just get a brief glance at this Hawk.

Mid-April to mid-September.

Northern Harrier*

Formerly called Marsh Hawk, Harriers fly much lower than the two hawks above, usually just above the ground. They have long tails and a white rump patch. The male is gray in colour and the female is brown.

Early April to October.

American Kestrel

Formerly called Sparrow Hawk, our smallest Hawk feeds mostly on Grasshoppers. Often you can see them hovering in one spot, or watching the ground from a power line.

Mid-April to late September.

Killdeer*

The Killdeer is actually a plover, a shorebird, but it is often found far from water and has been known to nest on Nose Hill. It is distinguished by two brown bands across its breast and the loud and clear call it makes, "Killdeer, Killdeer".

Early March to early October.

Northern Flicker*

A spotted-breasted woodpecker with a black band across the front of the breast.

Early April to late September.

Eastern Kingbird

A common flycatcher, Robin-sized, dark above and white below.

Third week of May to late August.

Horned Lark*

One of the commonest birds on Nose Hill and one of the earliest to be seen in the spring. Sparrow-sized birds, they can often be seen in small flocks flitting about the prairie, although they do not commonly sit for long enough to be identified. If you do see one close up, you will see its distinctive features — a black band across the chest and another from the bill to the eye and curving below the eye.

Horned Lark

You may see some yellow above and below the bill and the small "horns" if you are lucky. Tail feathers are black except for a few outer ones which are white, a feature which you may notice especially when the bird is flying away.

Late February to late September. An occasional bird may overwinter.

Alder Flycatcher

Formerly called Traill's Flycatcher. This small gray bird is best identified by its two-syllable call "Three-beers". Nesting is probable.

Least Flycatcher

This small gray bird can generally only be identified by its repeated call "che-bek", "che-bek". It stays mostly in the Aspen woods. Nesting is probable.

The Alder and Least Flycatcher are difficult to tell apart in the field. Both have white eye rings and white wing bars, but the only reliable means of identification are the calls as mentioned above.

Third week of May to early September. Most birds have left by the end of August.

Bank Swallow*

You may see these swallows in large numbers entering their nesting holes on the edge of the gravel banks. A brown band across the breast is a distinctive feature. Other swallows such as the Tree Swallow, the Barn Swallow and the Northern Rough-winged Swallow may also be seen soaring over the hill, but these are usually visitors.

First half of May to the last half of August.

American Crow*

Crows are present in wooded valleys throughout the breeding season. They may be seen flying over in the fall, usually in large flocks.

Late March or early April to mid-October.

House Wren*

This small brownish bird (with lighter stripes on its rump) is the smallest bird you are likely to see on Nose Hill. It nests in the thickest Aspens and shrubbery.

Third week of May to late August or early September.

House Wren

Rock Wren

Nose Hill is the only spot in Calgary that these birds can be expected, as they prefer barren areas. It is slightly larger and paler than the House Wren.

Third week of May to late August.

Gray Catbird   *American Robin*

Gray Catbird

This bird does sound somewhat like a cat, but it is very secretive, and generally not seen. It is usually hidden in the thickest part of the Aspen woods, and is not common.

Third week of May to early or mid-September.

American Robin*

This red-breasted bird is the one most people know from their own back yards. It thrives on Nose Hill, nesting in the Aspens.

Mid to late March to October.

Sprague's Pipit

This sparrow-sized bird is often heard singing over grasslands south and west of Porcupine Valley. It is rare to see one close up, so you must rely on their distinctive song for identification — a series of notes descending in frequency.

Yellow Warbler*

This is a small, almost pure yellow bird (no black). It can usually be found in shrubbery or Aspens. It has a distinctive song, which descends in frequency.

Mid-May to late August.

Western Meadowlark*

A very noticeable resident of the prairies, it is a yellow bird with a black band across its chest and a beautiful song. They can often be seen and heard singing from a fence post.

Late March to mid-October.

Northern (Baltimore) Oriole*

The male is an orange-breasted bird with a black head, found in small numbers in the Aspen woods. It has a loud call. The female is yellow-orange-breasted and lacks the black head of the male. Not a common bird, but colourful when seen.

Third week of May to the third week of August.

Northern (Baltimore) Oriole

Western Meadowlark

Brewer's Blackbird*

The male is a shiny blackbird with a light eye, and the female is dark brown with a dark brown eye. They nest where the grasses are thickest, and travel in flocks on migration. They are found most often in the east end of Porcupine Valley.

Early May to the end of September.

Brown-headed Cowbird*

The male resembles a Blackbird (with a brown head) but has a shorter bill and tail. The female is a plain brownish-gray. They lay their eggs in other birds' nests, primarily those of Warblers and native Sparrows.

Lazuli Bunting*

The male has a blue head, back and tail, with white wing bars. The female is plain with blueish feathers only on the rump and tail. It could not be considered a common bird, but is mentioned because of its first known breeding in 1985, and again in 1986, when a nest with young was found on the south-facing slopes.

American Goldfinch

The male is a pure yellow bird with black on its wings, and on the top of the head. They have a roller-coaster flight and often sing when flying.

Late May to late September.
Nesting is probable.

Savannah Sparrow*

A common Sparrow of the grasslands. The field marks are a streaked breast, a short tail and a yellow stripe above the eyes, although the latter is sometimes pale. The best way to tell the Savannah Sparrow is by its song — two short

American Goldfinch

Brewer's Blackbird

notes followed by a longer higher trill which seems as if the bird is having trouble getting it out.

Late April to mid or late September.

Vesper Sparrow*

The Vesper Sparrow is one of the commonest grassland sparrows on Nose Hill. It also has a streaked breast, but is paler than the Savannah Sparrow. Another distinctive feature is the white outer tail feathers. Often the best way to tell the Vesper Sparrow is by its beautiful song, which begins with four notes followed by a trill.

Late April to August.

Chipping Sparrow*

This small sparrow with its rusty cap and unstreaked breast can be found feeding in the grasslands, although it nests in Willow shrubs and Aspen groves.

First half of May to mid to late September.

Clay-coloured Sparrow*

This fairly common sparrow also has an unstreaked breast, but otherwise has no distinguishing features except for its song which is a series of buzzes.

Early May to mid to late September.

Lincoln's Sparrow*

This small sparrow with a finely-streaked breast is usually found singing in woodland valleys. It is best identified by its song, a loud series of trills.

Third week of May to late September and early October.

Further Reading

Godfrey, W. Earl 1986 *The Birds of Canada.* National Museums of Canada. Bulletin No. 203. Information Canada, Ottawa, Ontario
Salt, W. Ray and A.L. Wilk 1976 *The Birds of Alberta.* The Queen's Printer, Edmonton, Alberta

Peterson, Roger Tory 1961 *A Field Guide to Western Birds.* Houghton Mifflin Company, Boston, Massachusetts

Robbins, Chandler S., Bertel Bruun, Herbert S. Zim and Arthur Singer 1983 *Birds of North America.* Golden Press, New York, New York

National Geographic Society 1983 *Field Guide to the Birds of North America.* National Geographic Society, Washington, D.C.

Mammals
Herta Przeczek

Characteristics of Mammals

Mammals are the most highly-evolved group of the Vertebrates: animals with backbones. Their young are born alive; this is an important factor in their success because the unborn young are protected inside the body of the mother, in an ideal environment. When the young are born, they are fed on milk from the mother's mammary glands, hence the name "mammals", so the young get an excellent start in life.

Mammals are warm-blooded. This gives them another great advantage over groups such as the reptiles that are cold-blooded, because they are less affected by changes of temperature in their environment. Snakes, for example, become sluggish when the temperature falls below a certain point; they cannot live in the Arctic, but the Polar Bears, the Arctic Fox and Walruses can live there all through the year; these are all mammals.

Another characteristic of mammals is the fact that their bodies are often covered with hair. There are some exceptions, such as Armadillos and Whales; humans have lost much of the hairy covering.

Mammals have become adapted to many different environments; this adaptability is another factor in their success. They are found on land, for example, Bears, Elephants and Coyotes; they are found flying in the air, for example, Bats. Some live in the sea, like Whales, and some, like Moles, live under the earth.

Brief Glossary

Altrical: requiring long parental care after birth.
Precocious: requiring short periods of parental care after birth.
Fossorial: adapted for living totally or partially underground.
Forbs: soft-stemmed plants found on the prairie, suitable for forage.
Crepuscular: active during dawn and dusk.
Semi-plantigrade: walking on the heel, partly or sometime.

Mammals of Nose Hill

Seventeen mammals have been recorded for Nose Hill. Some of them are common residents, others are scarce residents, while others are only visitors. One of them, the Buffalo, is no longer present.

American Badger *Taxidea taxus*

American Badger

A scarce resident. A large member of the weasel family, it has a stout body with short ears, legs and tail. It has broad semi-plantigrade feet with extremely long ivory-coloured claws on the forefeet. It has a small head, broad between the ears, tapering to a pointed snout. The badger's head has a very distinctive pattern. The muzzle, crown and hind neck are dark green to almost black; the whole area is divided by a narrow white mid-dorsal line, which runs from muzzle to shoulder. This white line is matched on each side of the face by white cheeks and white ears trimmed with black. Behind the eye on each cheek is a black crescentic spot.

Habits. Primarily a fossorial animal, it is a powerful digger and a courageous fighter. Solitary dwellers, they are unusual for the weasel family as they hibernate in the winter from November to April. They are primarily nocturnal, but may be observed sunning near their burrows. They live in large burrows which can be as long as thirty feet and ten feet deep, situated on the open prairie. The entrances are obvious because of the great mounds of excavated earth. Bulky nests of grasses are constructed at the ends of the burrows. Badgers often take over and enlarge the burrows of Prairie Dogs and Ground Squirrels. Their food consists of Ground Squirrels, Pocket Gophers, Prairie Dogs, Mice and Voles. They also eat ground-nesting Birds, Snails and Insects. The Badger has developed a unique hunting method. It digs into a back entrance of a Ground Squirrel burrow, enlarges it to within about a foot of the entrance to fit its body, blocks the rear entrance with dirt and then lies concealed until an unwary animal rushes into the burrow and its waiting jaws. The Badgers are too powerful and too-quick diggers to have any predator but man. They have a unique hunting partnership with the Coyote.

Habitat. Open prairies, farmlands and parklands. One was sighted on Nose Hill, May 11, 1982.

Reproduction. Mating occurs between August and September, and implantation of the embryo is delayed until about mid-February. The young average four, and are born between late April and mid-May. Young Badgers romp playfully around the mouth of the den in the early summer. They are weaned when half-grown; they are brought food by the mother until they are nearly adult.

Little Brown Bat   *Myotis lucifugus*

A rare summer visitor, abundance unknown. It was observed in 1971 and 1972.

Bison   *Bison bison*

A hundred years ago Buffalo were probably still present on Nose Hill. Their trails and rubbing stones can still be seen.

Coyote   *Canis latrans*

It is dog-like in appearance and size with a slender pointed nose, erect ears, bushy tail with black tip. The lengthy thick hair is mostly grayish. Average weight 12 kg.

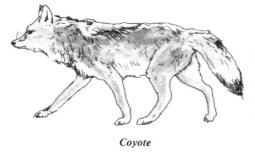

Coyote

Habits. This shrewd and clever predator is a skillful hunter operating singly or in pairs. They fashion burrows for retreat, seclusion and propagation. These can be found on the open prairies, hillsides of draws and coulees, and in the woods. Often their howls can be heard in the night or pre-dawn hours. The eerie repertoire of the coyote includes haunting bursts of yodelling and yapping. Most of the time their diet consists of birds, rodents, hares, grasshoppers, reptiles, berries and carrion. They are capable of pulling down calves of hoofed animals.

Habitat. The coyote is an adaptable animal and is one of the few native animals that have been able to adjust to human settlement. They can be found in alpine tundra, boreal forest, Aspen parkland and short-grass prairie. They prefer hilly country with Poplar bluffs and Willow-lined stream banks. On Nose Hill they are occasionally seen or heard in the grasslands area, and in Porcupine Valley.

Reproduction. The coyote is deemed to be monogamous. The mating season occurs late in February, the gestation period is 63 days. Five to seven whelps are born in late April. They are born blind, and by the time they are five to six weeks old they are able to leave the den and play nearby like puppies. By August they run with their parents and learn the arts of hunting and self-preservation.

Mule Deer *Odocoileus hemionus*

An uncommon resident. A large and stocky animal with large ears, and a short cylindrical tail, black-tipped. The dew-claws are situated high on the slender foot. Pelage is rather coarse, and the summer coat is reddish brown or tawny. It has a moist muzzle. Their winter coat is longer and thicker and has underfur. Bucks shed their antlers in spring between January and mid-April.

Habits. Mule deer are gregarious. Small groups of does and bucks band together in summer. In winter, they form large mixed bands of all ages and even associate with herds of Wapiti and Pronghorn. An experienced doe is the leader. Mule Deer have a special stiff-legged bounding gait which has led to them being called Jumping Deer. They undertake seasonal altitudinal migrations. Their winter diet is composed of twigs from trees and shrubs; favourites include Aspen, Willow and Red Osier Dogwood. In spring and summer grasses predominate. Predators of the species are Coyote and Lynx.

Habitats are open coniferous forest, subclimax brush, Aspen parkland, steep broken terrain and river valleys. On Nose Hill they can be found in the Aspen parkland and shrub communities.

Reproduction. The rut occurs between late October and early December. Bucks are truculent and dangerous during this period. They exhibit typical ungulate male rutting stance. The gestation period is 210 days and fawns are usually born in early June. Twins are common. Does cache their fawns for the first month, and they are weaned after four to five months.

White-tailed Deer *Odocoilous virginianus*

A scarce resident. This Deer has a slender graceful body, with slim legs,

Mule Deer

White-tailed Deer

small dew-claws high on each side of the foot, hooves narrow and pointed. The tail is almost a foot long, with a broad base, brown above with a wide white fringe; the deer flops it from side to side, or waves it high over the back, exposing the snowy white undersurface. Summer coat is thin and reddish-fawn with white on belly. The winter coat is longer and stiffer, grizzled-grey.

Habits. White-tailed deer are generally solitary, especially in the summer. In winter, bands may be formed and are usually led by a doe. They are quick to note movement but slow to recognize stationary objects. They are twilight creatures, active at dawn and dusk, and they bed down for the night. During the winter they yard up and form well-marked trails. They are static and will occupy a home range, and will be very reluctant to leave it. In mountainous areas they undertake altitudinal migrations. They are browsers living on buds and twigs of shrubs and saplings in the winter, and in the summer they supplement their diet with tender young grass and fruit in the autumn. They prefer Red Osier Dogwood, Aspen and Poplar. Their summer diet includes the forbs of Lambs-quarters, Asters and Goldenrod. They also consider Mushrooms a delicacy. The Coyote is a serious predator in the west.

Habitat. On the prairies they shelter in wooded coulees during the day and forage on the open prairie during twilight hours. On Nose Hill they have been observed in Aspen groves and shrub communities.

Reproduction. The rutting season occurs between mid-October and late December. Bucks thrash bushes with their antlers and joust with other bucks. The gestation period is approximately 210 days. Does pick sheltered spots, such as shrub-covered valleys, to drop their fawns, sometime between April and September. Twins are usually born. New-born fawns have bright reddish silky coats dappled with quarter-sized spots on flanks. They can stand within a few hours. The doe caches each one separately. Fawns are odourless for the first week so Coyotes cannot find them. They are weaned at four months but can graze and run agilely at three months.

Northern Plains Red Fox   *Vulpes fulva regalis*
A rare visitor. One was seen on August 20, 1973.

Richardson Pocket Gopher   *Thomomys talpoides talpoides*
It is a thickset, short-tailed fossorial rodent, with a blunt face, small eyes, extremely small round ears and short legs. Forelimbs are armed with four long, strong curved claws adapted for digging, and it has a short, thick, nearly naked tail. This possesses specialized sensitivity, which enables the gopher to feel its way in tunnels and to run rapidly in reverse. The most unusual features are the ample fur-lined cheek pouches which extend backwards to the shoulder. They have large prominent incisor teeth which protrude, and help them in cutting roots

without getting soil in their mouths. Pelage is soft and thick, short with a silky sheen. The back is generally brown, flanks are grey, belly is a buffy grey and the chin is white.

Habitat. Natural grasslands, cultivated fields and roadsides. They prefer a deep, heavy moist soil and in the summer they can be found on the edges of Aspen groves. On Nose Hill they can be found only by the evidence of their plugged burrows. They are rarely seen, as they travel by night.

Habits. Pocket gophers are active all year in their burrows. Their tunnel system consists of two levels. They have two deep permanent galleries, six to nine feet underground, which contain several nesting chambers and storage areas. The shallow feeding-tunnels are at a depth of five to eighteen inches. The gopher uses its powerful front claws to excavate and its hind legs to kick the earth backwards and then bulldozes the earth to the surface. It always plugs the entrances with a firm earth plug. In summer they eat the stems and leaves of green plants. (They secure their food in nocturnal forays.) Their favorite plants are Dandelions, Pea Vine, Sage, Clover, Anemone, Goldenrod, Yarrow and Penstemon. They cut the roots and grasses into short lengths and stuff them into their cheek pouches with their forefeet. They empty their pouches by placing their forepaws at the back of the pouches and pushing forward. They collect roots for winter storage.

They are prey for Badgers, Weasel, Coyotes, and nocturnal predators, such as the Great Horned Owl.

Reproduction. Breeding season occurs from April to early May. Young Gophers are born in late May. Litter size averages 2 or 3. They are born blind and toothless, and cheek pouches appear two days later. The young leave the nest about August and travel above ground some distance before digging their own burrows. They suffer a heavy mortality rate at this time.

Under natural conditions they perform a useful role in the ecology of grasslands. They keep soil porous and arable by burrowing up arable subsoil and scattering it on the surface. They turn over 3-6 tons of soil per acre, and they enrich the soil by burying vegetation which later forms humus. Their consumption of forbs assists in the establishment of turf.

White-tailed Hare   *Lepus townsendii campanius*

This is a relatively slim hare with very slender long legs, long ears and a long white tail. In summer it is grizzled buffy grey. The winter coat is pure white, with black-tipped ears.

Habits. When disturbed this Hare flees with high, long jumps. This is why it is usually referred to as a Jack Rabbit. It has been estimated that it travels as fast as forty miles an hour. It is also a very strong swimmer and is the least sociable of the Hares. In summer these Hares crouch in shallow depressions and in the winter they burrow under the snow to make snow tunnels and snow caves. They huddle in these, out of the biting wind and cold. They like extensive semi-open thickets where they hide from their enemies. Their food consists of a wide range of vegetable matter including wild grasses, Clover and leaves of native and cultivated shrubbery. In winter they are often driven to feed on the bark and twigs of shrubs, and pillage Alfalfa fields, stacks of hay, green feed and unharvested grain. Jack Rabbits serve as prey for a number of prairie predators including Coyotes, large Hawks and by night, the larger Owls.

Habitat. Pastures, cultivated fields, borders of Willow thickets and Wild Rose tangles, also mature short-grass plains. They are found on Nose Hill in the grasslands and shrub communities.

Reproduction. Their mating season is early in May. The young are born in a shallow nest hidden in grass or in an abandoned Badger burrow. The young are born sometime in May, are heavily furred, and their eyes are open. Litters average four, and the new-born can run.

Varying Hare - Snowshoe Hare *Lepus americanus americanus*

An uncommon resident. It is medium-sized and weighs four pounds, has large broad hind feet and large ears. Summer pelage is a grizzled rusty or greying-brown with a white belly. The tail is blackish. In winter the hare turns white except for the eyelids and tips of the ears which are black. The large hind feet are padded with thick stiff hairs which give it its popular name — Snowshoe Hare.

Habits. It is crepuscular and nocturnal in its activity patterns and remains active all winter. Because of its protective coloration, the hare may freeze to escape detection or may flee in long bounds that cover ten feet, at speeds up to twenty-seven miles an hour. They follow familiar runways which in summer are well-padded trails tunnelled through fresh grass. In winter they are well-marked padded trails in the snow.

White-tailed Hare

Varying Hare - Snowshoe Hare

Their senses are extremely acute. In summer they eat a variety of forbs and green grasses, Wild Strawberry, Pussy-toes, Dandelion, Clover and Daisies. They also eat the tender leaves of the Trembling Aspen, Birches and Willows. In winter they live on buds, twigs and bark.

Habitat. In the prairie region they inhabit Aspen groves. They like to remain in the dense cover of thickets during the day. On Nose Hill they are restricted to dense thickets and Aspen groves.

They have many predators, chief among them the large Owls, and Coyotes.

Reproduction. Breeding season starts in late March and often begins with curious courtship parades. The doe may produce as many as four litters a year. Average litter size is four. The young are born with a long coat of silky grizzled-brown hair in a grass-lined nest. Their eyes open soon after birth, and by the sixth day they can hop away from the nest and begin to eat green plants.

Lynx *Lynx canadensis canadensis*

A rare visitor. A Lynx was seen in the western section of Nose Hill in 1972.

Muskrat *Ondatra zibethicus cinnamoninus*

A rare visitor. One was seen in a pond in 1972 north of 53rd Street N.W.

Porcupine *Erethizon dorsatum epixanthum*

A scarce resident. A large spiny sluggish rodent, Canada's second largest rodent, 90 cm long, approximately 12 kg, with a robust body, small head, blunt muzzles and a very thick tail. It has short strong legs with powerful long curved black claws. The pelage consists of dense woolly brown undercoat, long cream-tipped guard hairs, and stiff quills. The quills and hair can be erected in defence. It has been estimated a porcupine has 30,000 quills.

Habits. Porcupines are solitary and cantankerous. They shuffle along the ground, and if alarmed they will break into a slow lumbering gallop. In winter they plow trenches in the soft snow because of their short legs. They are excellent swimmers and climbers. They are well-known for their unique mode of defence. It is often thought that they throw their quills but this is not so. They deliver a lightning-fast blow with their tails and the lateral quills are easily left impaled in the attacker. They make use of ground shelters such as road culverts, hollow logs and brush piles. In winter they make snow tunnels leading to their

Porcupine

retreats. Their diet consists of a variety of lush green leaves of forbs, shrubs and trees. They are fond of the Aspen. In winter they feed on the cambium layer and inner bark of trees as well as new twigs and buds.

Habitat. They are found in both deciduous and coniferous forested regions, and, especially in summer, they are found on the prairies. On Nose Hill they are occasionally seen in Porcupine Valley, in Aspen groves and dense shrubbery.

Reproduction. Porcupines mate in November or December and the pair indulge in a comical rough-house dance. The young are born from mid-May to the end of June, and only one Porcupine is born. The young are precocious, are covered with long black hair, and quills about one inch long; these quills are soft and limp at birth. Their eyes are open and they can walk briskly in a very short time. In marked contrast to their stolid elders they are very playful. The young porcupines follow their mothers and are weaned after their second week. They tag along with her, sampling green foliage.

Richardson Ground Squirrel   *Citellus richardsonii richardsonii*

The Richardson Ground Squirrel is a plump-bodied species about 30 cm long with short legs, armed with long, slightly curved claws. The

general colour is a buffy yellow, shaded over the back with fine irregular grayish mottlings. Its ears are very small, and its tail is short and stubby, about a third of the body length. They have small internal cheek pouches. Average weight is 350 grams.

Richardson Ground Squirrel

Habits. They are observable from April to November, and are harbingers of spring. They emerge late in March to stand erect on their hind legs like sentinels. They scurry from hole to hole emitting shrill whistles to warn neighbours that strangers are present. They are remarkable winter sleepers and spend the cold Calgary winter, from late October to March, in a deep coma in underground burrows. During this time they slowly absorb the accumulated fat stored during the previous Autumn. They also subsist on underground stores of seeds and grains. They are largely herbivorous with a very active appetite, and eat roots, bulbs, stems, leaves, seeds of grasses and some herbaceous plants. They will also feed on insects, bird's eggs and even young birds. The Ground Squirrel is often referred to, incorrectly, as a "Gopher" which comes from the French word for honeycomb (gaufre): a very appropriate reference to its burrows. They live in loose straggling colonies and excavate complicated burrows which consist of a maze of galleries, entrances and chambers.

They fall prey to a host of predators which includes most of the Hawk species. Among the four-footed predators are the Long-tailed Weasel,

Badger, and the Coyote.

Habitat. They inhabit open prairie and prefer rolling hills of gravelly or sandy soils in which to burrow. They are quick to move into cultivated fields, and avoid wetlands. On Nose Hill they can be found in the grasslands. A large colony was found in May 1987 near the 64 Avenue ravine.

Reproduction. Mating takes place during April. After a gestation period of 28 to 32 days, the females give birth to six to eleven young. They are born in underground dens during late April to May. By late May or early June, the young can be seen romping and feeding close to the burrows.

Meadow Vole *Microtus pennsylvanicus drummondii*

It is medium-sized, short-bodied and has small beady eyes, rounded ears and a short tail. It is often referred to as a Field Mouse. Its summer coat is short, rough, rusty-brown above and greyish underneath. Its winter coat is silkier, longer and greyer than its summer coat. Average length, 144-197 mm, average weight, 30-40 grams.

Habits. Voles are clean creatures and spend much time grooming and washing their faces. They use a communal toilet some distance away from their nests. They are most active during the hours of dawn to dusk, and they make clearly-defined runways or vole highways in overgrown meadows. They gnaw off grass stems and then trample down paths. The grass growing on each side eventually arches over the runways providing added security. In winter the runways are still used under the heavy blankets of snow. They weave nests out of grasses, and in the summer eat sedges, flowers and leaves. In winter they eat seeds, underground roots and bulbs. The roots of the Three-flowered Avens are a favorite food on the prairies as well as seeds of Brome and Crested Wheatgrass.

Habitat. The preferred habitat of the Meadow Vole is wet meadow, but the species will inhabit any grassland habitat, large or small. On Nose Hill it is found in the shrubbery and grasslands areas. Voles are one of the most important food sources for a legion of predators, including Weasels, Badgers, Foxes, Coyotes, Crows, Magpies, Hawks and Gulls.

Reproduction. Breeding starts in April and continues until October. Three to five litters are born to a single female, and litter size varies between one and eleven. Voles are born blind, deaf, and helpless. After five or six days they are clothed in velvety fur, and they are weaned on the twelfth day. Soon afterwards they scatter from the natal nest.

Meadow Vole

Least Weasel   *Mustela nivalis rixosa*

Rare. On January 10, 1987, Catharine Osborne (CFNS member) saw a Least Weasel at the Communications Tower site in the gravel pit area of Nose Hill.

The Least Weasel is one of the smallest carnivores. It is scarcely larger than its prey — it seldom exceeds 8 inches.

Its habits and habitat are similar to those of the other weasel species.

It is capable of producing four litters each summer.

Prairie Long-tailed Weasel   *Mustela frenata longicauda*

It is a small carnivore with a slender sinuous body, lithe and strong. Its fur is smooth, compact and glossy, and it has a small head, low, round, swept-back ears, and a black-tipped tail. Summer pelage is snuff-brown with white undersides. In winter it is completely white except for its black tail. It is the largest of our weasels.

Prairie Long-tailed Weasel

Habits. They commonly take over the burrows of Ground Squirrels or Pocket Gophers and adapt them to their own use. They use fur, feathers, dry grasses and shredded leaves to line their nests. Other parts of their burrows consist of larder and toilet areas. As winter approaches they begin to amass an underground larder full of mice. Some build dens in hollow logs, under roots, and in abandoned machinery and farm buildings. They are admirably suited for killing small mammals. They make quick dashes to capture their prey, grab them by the neck and bite through. They cling tenaciously to larger animals, with their teeth and stubby legs, and wrap their slim bodies around their prey very much like a snake. They eat Hares, Ground Squirrels, Voles and Mice. They will also eat young ground-nesting birds, and are known for their predation of chicken coops. They also eat Grasshoppers and Flies. They are in turn preyed upon by Foxes, Coyotes, domestic Cats and Dogs.

Habitat. They show a preference for open country grasslands, Aspen parkland and river-bottom land. On Nose Hill they are occasionally seen in the grassland and Aspen groves.

Reproduction. Both sexes are sexually inactive while the winter coat is worn. Mating occurs July, August, and implantation of the embryos is delayed from September until March. Gestation period is approximately 27 days and the young are weaned at 3½ weeks. The female then takes the young hunting. The average litter size is six.

Disturbance By Man

Due to extensive habitat disturbances, the frequency, density and distribution of the known mammal population of Nose Hill has undergone widespread changes since 1981.

Further Reading

Banfield, A.W.F. 1974 *The Mammals of Canada.* University of Toronto Press, Toronto, Ontario
Bird, C.D. (Ed.) 1974 *Natural Areas 1973.* Calgary Field Naturalists' Society, P.O. Box 981, Calgary, Alberta
Pinel, Harold W. (Ed.) 1981 *Calgary's Natural Areas.* The Calgary Field Naturalists' Society, P.O. Box 981, Calgary, Alberta
Soper, S.D. 1964 *The Mammals of Alberta.* Flamby Press, Edmonton, Alberta

Check List

The following lists include all of the living organisms which have been observed and recorded as occurring on Nose Hill. Many uncommon or otherwise obscure organisms are listed here which are not described in the book.

Key

Common names of organisms described in the text are set in **bold type.**

★   indicates organisms observed and recorded after publication of the 1981 *Calgary's Natural Areas.*

☆   indicates organisms which are common in Calgary, but not frequently seen on Nose Hill.

A single character grades frequency of occurrence as follows:
1   rare
2   occasional
3   common
4   abundant
+   present

For birds a two-character annotation describes status and relative occurrence as follows:

R   permanent resident
S   summer resident
W   winter resident
M   migrant

1 = rarely — less than annual
2, 3, 4 = annually
2 = fewer than 6
3 = 6 to 25
4 = more than 25

This is followed by an asterisk ("*") for species known to nest on the hill.

Vascular plants

Nomenclature follows Packer, *Flora of Alberta*. The plant names in parentheses are the names used by E.H. Moss in the previous edition.

Ferns and Fern-like Allies

Selaginella densa
Little Club Moss 3

Conifers

★ ☆ *Juniperus horizontalis*
Creeping Juniper 1
★ ☆ *Picea glauca*
White Spruce..................................1

Monocots

Agropyron pectiniforme (A. cristatum)
Crested Wheat Grass 3
A. dasystachyum (A. riparium)
Wheat Grass 2
A. smithii var. *molle*
Western Wheat Grass............................2
Agrostis stolonifera (A. alba)
Redtop......................................2
A. scabra
Hair Grass...................................2
Allium cernuum
Nodding Onion...............................2
A. textile
Prairie Onion 2
Beckmannia syzigachne
Slough Grass.................................2
Bouteloua gracilis
Blue Grama 3
Bromus inermis ssp. *inermis*
Awnless Brome...............................3
B. inermis ssp. *pumpellianus (B. pumpellianus)*
Northern Awnless Brome 2
Calamagrostis inexpansa
Northern Reed Grass 2

Calamovilfa longifolia
Sand Grass 3
Carex atherodes
Awned Sedge.................................2
C. filifolia
Thread-leaved Sedge 2
C. sprengelii
Sprengel's Sedge.............................2
Danthonia parryi
Parry Oat Grass 3
Disporum trachycarpun
Fairy Bells 2
Eleocharis acicularis
Needle Spike Rush 3
Festuca scabrella
Rough Fescue 3
Habenaria hyperborea
Northern Green Bog Orchid 1
H. viridis var. *bracteata*
Bracted Orchid 2
Helictotrichon hookeri
Hooker's Oat Grass 2
Hierachloe odorata
Sweet Grass...............................3
Hordeum jubatum
Foxtail Barley 3
Juncus balticus var. *montanus*
Wire Rush 3
Koeleria macrantha (K. cristata)
June Grass.................................3
Lilium philadelphicum var. *andinum*
Western Wood Lily 2
Phalaris arundinacea
Reed Canary Grass............................1
Phleum pratense
Timothy.....................................2
Poa compressa
Canada Bluegrass.............................2
P. interior
Inland Bluegrass..............................2
P. pratensis
Kentucky Bluegrass 3
Sisyrinchium montanum
Blue-eyed Grass 2
S. septentrionale (S. sarmentosum)
Pale Blue-eyed Grass 1

Smilacina racemosa var. *amplexicaulis*
  False Solomon's Seal 2
S. stellata
  Star-flowered Solomon's Seal.....................3
Stipa columbiana
  Columbia Needle Grass 2
S. comata
  Spear Grass......................................2
S. spartea var. *curtiseta*
  Porcupine Grass 2
S. viridula
  Green Needle Grass 2
Zygadenus elegans
  White Camas.....................................3
Z. venenosus var. *gramineus (Z. gramineus)*
  Death Camas...................................2

Dicots

Achillea millefolium var. *lanulosa*
  Common Yarrow 4
Agoseris glauca
  False Dandelion 3
Alyssum alyssoides
  Small Alyssum 1
Amelanchier alnifolia
  Saskatoon 3
Androsace septentrionalis
  Fairy Candelabra 3
Anemone canadensis
  Canada Anemone...............................3
A. cylindrica
  Long-fruited Anemone 2
A. multifida
  Cut-leaved Anemone 3
A. patens
  Prairie Crocus..................................4
Antennaria parvifolia (A. nitida)
  Small-leaved Pussytoes 2
A. pulcherrima
  Showy Everlasting 1
A. rosea
  Pink Pussytoes 2
Apocynum androsaemifolium
  Spreading Dogbane 3

Arabis hirsuta
Hirsute Rock Cress............................3
A. holboellii
Reflexed Rock Cress 3
Arctium minus
Common Burdock 2
★ ☆ *Arctostaphylos uva-ursi*
Common Bearberry 1
Arenaria congesta var. *lithophila*
Sandwort.....................................1
Arnica fulgens
Shining Arnica 2
A. lonchophylla
Spear-leaved Arnica..........................2
Artemisia campestris
Plains Sagewort 2
A. frigida
Pasture Sage 3
A. ludoviciana var. *gnaphalodes*
Prairie Sage................................3
Aster laevis
Smooth Aster 3
Aster ericoides ssp. *pansus (A. pansus)*
Tufted White Prairie Aster 3
A. falcatus
Creeping White Prairie Aster 1
Astragalus dasyglottis (A. agrestis)
Field or Purple Milk Vetch 2
A. crassicarpus
Buffalo Bean; Ground Plum....................3
A. miser var. *serotinus (A. decumbens* var. *serotinus)*
Timber Milk Vetch............................2
A. flexuosus
Slender Milk Vetch............................1
A. missouriensis
Missouri Milk Vetch...........................1
A. pectinatus
Narrow-leaved Milk Vetch 1
A. striatus
Ascending Purple Milk Vetch 2
Axyris amaranthoides
Russian Pigweed..............................2
☆ *Betula occidentalis*
Water Birch..................................1
Brassica juncea
Indian Mustard...............................2

B. kaber
Charlock; Wild Mustard 2
Campanula rotundifolia
Bluebell; Harebell 3
Capsella bursa-pastoris
Shepherd's-purse 2
Caragana arborescens
Caragana 2
★ *Carduus nutans*
Nodding Thistle 2
Carum carvi
Caraway 1
Castilleja miniata
Common Red Paintbrush 1
C. cusickii and *C. lutescens (C. septentrionalis)*
Common Yellow Paintbrush 2
Cerastium arvense
Chickweed 2
Chamaerhodos erecta ssp. *nuttallii*
Chamaerhodos 2
Chenopodium album
Lamb's-quarters 2
Cirsium arvense
Canada Thistle 3
C. undulatum
Wavy-leaved Thistle 3
C. vulgare
Bull Thistle 3
Clematis tangutica
Yellow Clematis 1
Collomia linearis
Collomia 1
Comandra umbellata var. *pallida (C. pallida)*
Pale Comandra 3
Cornus stolonifera
Red Osier Dogwood 3
Cotoneaster acutifolia
Cotoneaster 1
Crataegus rotundifolia (C. chrysocarpa)
Hawthorn 3
Crepis tectorum
Annual Hawksbeard 2
Cymopterus acaulis
Plains Cymopterus 1
Cynoglossum officinale
Hound's-tongue 3

Descurainia richardsonii
Grey Tansy Mustard 1
D. sophia
Flixweed 2
Diplotaxis muralis
Sand Rocket 2
Dodecatheon conjugens
Shooting Star 1
D. pulchellum (D. radicatum)
Shooting Star 2
Draba borealis
Boreal Draba...................................1
D. cana (D. lanceolata)
Hoary Whitlow Grass 2
D. nemorosa
Annual Draba..................................
Elaeagnus commutata
Wolf Willow; Silverberry 3
Epilobium angustifolium
Fireweed 4
E. ciliatum ssp. *glandulosum (E. glandulosum)*
Northern Willow-herb 1
Erigeron caespitosus
Tufted Fleabane 3
E. compositus
Compound or Daisy Fleabane 2
E. glabellus
Smooth Fleabane 2
Eriogonum flavum
Yellow Umbrella Plant 3
Erucastrum gallicum
Dog Mustard...................................2
Erysimum cheiranthoides
Wormseed Mustard 2
E. inconspicuum
Small-flowered Rocket 3
Fragaria virginiana var. *glauca*
Wild Strawberry...............................3
Gaillardia aristata
Gaillardia; Brown-eyed Susan 3
Galeopsis tetrahit
Hemp Nettle 1
Galium boreale
Northern Bedstraw.............................3
Gaura coccinea
Scarlet Butterfly-weed 3

Geranium viscosissimum
 Sticky Purple Geranium 3
Geum aleppicum
 Yellow Avens 2
G. macrophyllum
 Yellow Avens 1
G. triflorum
 Three-flowered Avens 3
Glycyrrhiza lepidota
 Wild Licorice 1
Gutierrezia sarothrae
 Broomweed 3
Hackelia floribunda
 Large-flowered Stickseed 2
Hedysarum alpinum
 American Hedysarum; Alpine Hedysarum 3
H. boreale var. *mackenzii (H. mackenzii)*
 Northern Hedysarum; Mackenzie's Hedysarum 3
Helianthus subrhomboideus
 (H. laetiflorus var. *subrhomboideus)*
 Rhombic-leaved Sunflower 1
Heuchera richardsonii
 Alum-root 2
Heterotheca villosa (Chrysopsis villosa)
 Golden Aster 3
Hieracium umbellatum (H. canadense)
 Canada Hawkweed 2
Lappula squarrosa (L. echinata)
 Blue-bur 3
Lathyrus ochroleucus
 Yellow Pea Vine 3
L. venosus
 Purple Pea Vine 1
Lepidium densiflorum
 Common Peppergrass 3
Lesquerella arenosa
 Bladderpod 3
★ *Liatris punctata*
 Blazing Star...................................1
Linaria dalmatica
 Toad-flax.....................................2
L. vulgaris
 Butter-and-eggs 3
Linum lewisii
 Wild Blue Flax 3

L. rigidum
Yellow Flax 1
Lithospermum incisum
Incised Puccoon 3
L. ruderale
Woolly Gromwell 3
Lomatium foeniculaceum
Yellow Prairie Parsley 1
Lomatium macrocarpum
White Prairie Parsley 2
Lonicera tartarica
Tartarian Honeysuckle 1
Lupinus sericeus
Perennial Lupine 2
Lygodesmia juncea
Skeleton-weed 2
Medicago sativa
Alfalfa 2
Melilotus alba
White Sweet Clover 3
M. officinalis
Yellow Sweet Clover 3
Monarda fistulosa var. *menthaefolia*
Wild Bergamot 3
Monolepsis nuttalliana
Spear-leaved Goosefoot 3
Musineon divaricatum
Rough-seeded Musineon 2
Neslia paniculata
Ball Mustard 1
Orobanche fasciculata
Clustered Broomrape 1
Orthocarpus luteus
Owl-clover 2
Orthilia secunda (Pyrola secunda)
One-sided Wintergreen 1
Osmorhiza depauperata
Sweet Cicely 1
Oxytropis monticola ssp. *monticola*
(O. campestris var. *gracilis)*
Late Yellow Loco-weed 2
O. sericea var. *spicata*
Early Yellow Locoweed 2
O. splendens
Showy Locoweed 2

Paronychia sessiliflora
Low Whitlow-wort 2

Penstemon nitidus
Smooth Blue Beard-tongue 3

P. procerus
Slender Blue Beard-tongue 1

Perideridia gairdneri
Gairdner's Squaw-root 1

Petalostemon candidum
White Prairie Clover 2

P. purpureum
Purple Prairie Clover 3

Phlox hoodii
Moss Phlox 3

Plantago major
Common Plantain   2

★ *Polygala senega*
Seneca-root 1

Polygonum aviculare
Common Knotweed 2

P. convolvulus
Wild Buckwheat 2

Populus balsamifera
Balsam Poplar 1

Populus tremuloides
Aspen 4

Potentilla anserina
Silverweed 3

Potentilla arguta
White Cinquefoil 2

P. concinna
Early Cinquefoil 3

★ *P. finitima*
Cinquefoil 1

P. fruticosa
Shrubby Cinquefoil 3

P. gracilis
Graceful Cinquefoil 2

P. hippiana (P. effusa)
Branched Cinquefoil 2

P. norvegica
Rough Cinquefoil 1

P. pensylvanica
Prairie Cinquefoil 2

Prunus virginiana
Choke Cherry 4

Psoralea esculenta
Indian Bread-root.................................1
Pyrola asarifolia
Common Pink Wintergreen 2
Ranunculus abortivus
Small-flowered Buttercup 1
R. acris
Tall Buttercup...................................2
R. cardiophyllus
Heart-leaved Buttercup 3
R. cymbalaria
Alkali Buttercup.................................2
R. reptans (R. flammula)
Creeping Spearwort 1
R. rhomboideus
Prairie Buttercup 2
R. sceleratus
Cursed Crowfoot 1
Ribes oxyacanthoides
Wild Gooseberry 2
Rosa acicularis
Prickly Rose 2
R. woodsii
Common Wild Rose............................3
Rubus idaeus (R. strigosus)
Wild Red Raspberry.............................1
Rumex occidentalis
Western Dock 1
Salix bebbiana
Bebb's Willow.................................3
Senecio canus
Prairie Groundsel 3
Shepherdia canadensis
Canadian Buffalo-berry 2
Silene noctiflora
Night-flowering Catchfly 2
Sisymbrium altissimum
Tumbling Mustard 2
Sium suave
Water Parsnip...................................2
Solanum triflorum
Wild Tomato....................................1
Solidago gigantea
Late Goldenrod 3
S. missouriensis
Low Goldenrod 3

S. spathulata (S. decumbens)
Mountain Goldenrod 3
Sonchus asper
Annual Sow Thistle 1
Sorbus aucuparia
Mountain Ash 1
Sphaeralcea coccinea
Scarlet Mallow 2
Spiraea betulifolia (S. lucida)
White Meadowsweet 2
Stachys palustris ssp. *pilosa*
Hedge Nettle 2
Stellaria longipes
Long-stalked Chickweed 2
S. media
Common Chickweed 2
Symphoricarpos albus
Snowberry 2
S. occidentalis
Buckbrush 4
Taraxacum officinale
Common Dandelion 3
Thalictrum venulosum
Veiny Meadow Rue 2
Thermopsis rhombifolia
Golden Bean 4
Thlaspi arvense
Stinkweed 3
Tragopogon dubius
Goat's-beard 2
Urtica dioica ssp. *gracilis (U. gracilis)*
Common Nettle 2
Vicia americana (V. sparsifolia)
American Vetch; Wild Vetch 3
Viola adunca
Early Blue Violet 3
V. nuttallii
Yellow Prairie Violet 3
V. canadensis var. *rugulosa*
Western Canada Violet 3
V. pedatifida
Crowfoot Violet 2
Zizia aptera
Heart-leaved Alexanders 3

Non-Vascular Plants

Mushrooms and Slime Molds

    Agaricus sp. 2
    A. campestris 2
    Agrocybe dura 2
    Bisporella citrina . . . . +
★ **Bjerkandera adusta** 2
    Bovista plumbea 1
    Calvatia bovista var. **bovista** 2
    C. cyathiformis 3
    Chlorociboria aeruginascens 2
    Clitocybe geotropa 2
    C. praemagna 2
★ **Cortinarius** sp. 1
    Daedaleopsis confragosa 2
    Fuligo septica 1
    Geastrum floriformes 3
    Helvella sp. 1
★ **Inocybe** sp. 1
    Lycoperdon polymorphum 1
    L. umbrinum 1
    Marasmius epiphyllus 2
★ **M. oreades** 2
    Melanoleuca spp. 3
    Nectria cinnabarina 3
    Panaeolus separatus 2
    Peniophora polygonia 2
    P. rufa 2
★ **Phellinus tremulae** 2
    Phlebia strigosozonata 2
    Puccinia monoica 2
    Schizophyllum commune 3
    Stropharia semiglobata 2
    Trametes hirsuta 2
★ **Trichaptum biformis** 2
    Tubaria furfuracea 2
    Tulostoma simulans 2

Lichens

Tree Substrate
    Candelaria concolor 2

Evernia mesomorpha 2
Parmelia exasperatula 3
P. subolivacea 2
☆ *P. sulcata* 1
Physcia adscendens 3
P. aipolia 2
☆ *P. orbicularis* 1
P. stellaris 1
Rinodina mniaraea 1
Usnea compacta 2

Rotten Wood Substrate

Lecidea tornoensis 1
Xanthoria polycarpa 2

Soil Substrate

Buellia epigaea 2
Caloplaca jungermanniae 2
Cladonia pocillum 2
C. pyxidata 2
Collema tenax 1
Dermatocarpon hepaticum 2
Diploschistes scruposus 2
Lecidea decipiens 2
Peltigera rufescens 2
Toninia caeruleonigricans 2

Rock Substrate

Acarospora strigata 2
Caloplaca murorum 1
C. stillicidiorum 1
Dimelaena oreina 3
Lecanora alphoplaca 2
L. muralis 2
Rhizocarpon disporum 1
Xanthoria elegans 4

Mosses

Barbula acuta 2
Bryum argenteum 1
☆ *Brachythecium salebrosum* 2
Hypnum cupressiforme 2
Orthotrichum obtusifolium 2
Plagiomnium rugicum 1
Pterygoneurum sp 1
Pylaisiella polyantha 3

Tortula ruralis 3
Weissia controversa 1

Butterflies

Aglais milberti furcillata
  Milbert's Tortoiseshell 3
Agriades franklinii rustica
  Arctic Blue 2
Artogeia rapae
  Cabbage White 4
Basilarchia arthemis rubrofasciata
  White Admiral 2
Carterocephalus palaemon
  Arctic Skipper 1
Cercyonis pegala ino
  Large Wood Nymph 3
Charidryas gorgone carlota
  Gorgone Crescentspot 1
Clossiana bellona jenistae
  Meadow Fritillary 2
Coenonympha inornata benjamini
  Prairie Ringlet 3
Colias alexandra astraea
  Queen Alexandra's Sulphur 2
Colias philodice eriphyle
  Common Sulphur 4
Epidemia helloides
  Purplish Copper 2
Erebia discoidalis mcdunnoughi
  Red-disked Alpine 2
Erebia epipsodea
  Common Alpine 3
Erynnis icelus
  Dreamy Duskywing 2
Erynnis persius
  Persius Duskywing 3
Everes amyntula albrighti
  Western Tailed Blue 2
Glaucopsyche lygdamus couperi
  Silvery Blue 3
Harkenclenus titus immaculosus
  Coral Hairstreak 2
Hesperia comma assiniboia
  Common Branded Skipper 2

Icaricia acmon lutzi
Acmon Blue 1
Icaricia icarioides pembina
Common Blue.................................1
Incisalia augustus
Brown Elfin...................................1
Incisalia polios obscurus
Hoary Elfin 1
Lycaeides melissa
Melissa Blue 3
Nymphalis antiopa antiopa
Mourning Cloak 3
Oarisma garita
Garita Skipperling 3
Oeneis alberta
Alberta Arctic................................2
Oeneis uhleri varuna
Uhler's Arctic 2
Papilio zelicaon nitra
Anise Swallowtail............................1
Phyciodes pratensis
Field Crescentspot 1
P. tharos
Pearly Crescentspot 1
Plebejus saepiolus amica
Greenish Blue 3
Polites coras
Yellowpatch Skipper 2
P. draco
Draco Skipper...............................1
P. mystic dacotah
Long Dash...................................2
P.themistocles
Tawny-edged Skipper 1
Polygonia progne
Gray Comma 1
Pontia occidentalis
Western White 3
Pterourus glaucus canadensis
Tiger Swallowtail 2
Pyrgus communis
Common Checkered Skipper 2
Pyrgus ruralis
Two-banded Checkered Skipper................1
Speyeria aphrodite
Aphrodite 2

Speyeria atlantis beani
  Atlantis Fritillary 4
Speyeria callippe calgariana
  Callippe Fritillary 2
Speyeria cybele pseudocarpenteri
  Great Spangled Fritillary 2
Speyeria mormonia
  Mormon Fritillary 4
Vanessa atalanta rubria
  Red Admiral 2
Vanessa cardui
  Painted Lady 2

Birds

The following list covers the bird species seen more than once on, or
flying over, Nose Hill in the period 1976 to 1987 (since Calgary's
Natural Areas: A Popular Guide was published in 1975). It has been
compiled primarily from the notes of Jamey Podlubny and Ray
Woods. Ten species, all scarce or uncommon, seen prior to 1976, have
been omitted.

Canada Goose	M1
Mallard	S2
Pintail	M2
Northern Goshawk	M1
★ Cooper's Hawk	M1
Sharp-shinned Hawk	M1
Northern Harrier (Marsh Hawk)	S2*
Rough-legged Hawk	M2
Red-tailed Hawk	S2*
Swainson's Hawk	S2*
Golden Eagle	M1
Prairie Falcon	R2
Merlin (Pigeon Hawk)	R2
American Kestrel (Sparrow Hawk)	S2
Sharp-tailed Grouse	R2
Ring-necked Pheasant	R1
Gray Partridge	R3*
Killdeer	S3*
Marbled Godwit	M1
Long-billed Curlew	M1
Upland Sandpiper	M1
California Gull	S2
Ring-billed Gull	S3
Franklin's Gull	S2

Rock Dove (Pigeon) R3
Great Horned Owl R2*
★ Long-eared Owl S1*
Short-eared Owl S1
Northern Flicker S2*
Downy Woodpecker R2
★ **Alder Flycatcher** S2
Least Flycatcher S2
Eastern Kingbird S2
Say's Phoebe M1
Horned Lark S4*
Barn Swallow S2
Tree Swallow S2
Bank Swallow S4*
Rough-winged Swallow S2
Black-billed Magpie R3*
Common Raven W2
American Crow S3*
Black-capped Chickadee R3
House Wren S2*
Rock Wren S2
Gray Catbird S2
Brown Thrasher S1
American Robin S3*
Mountain Bluebird M1
★ Golden-crowned Kinglet M2
Ruby-crowned Kinglet M2
Water Pipit M3
Sprague's Pipit S2
Bohemian Waxwing W4
Cedar Waxwing S2
Northern Shrike M1
European Starling R4*
★ Red-eyed Vireo S2
Yellow Warbler S2*
Yellow-rumped Warbler M3
★ Palm Warbler M1
★ Wilson's Warbler M2
House Sparrow R2
Western Meadowlark S3*
Red-winged Blackbird M1
Brewer's Blackbird S3*
Brown-headed Cowbird S2
Northern (Baltimore) Oriole S2*
★ **Lazuli Bunting** S2*
★ Pine Grosbeak W1

    Hoary Redpoll W1
    Common Redpoll W3
    Pine Siskin.......................................M2
    American Goldfinch S3
    Rufous-sided Towhee S1
    Savannah Sparrow S3*
★   **Baird's Sparrow** S2
★   Le Conte's Sparrow S2
    Vesper Sparrow S3*
    Dark-eyed Junco...............................M3
    American Tree Sparrow.........................M3
    Chipping Sparrow S3
    Clay-coloured Sparrow S3*
    White-crowned Sparrow M2
    White-throated Sparrow M2
★   **Lincoln's Sparrow** S2*
    Song Sparrow M2
★   Lapland Longspur M4
    Snow Bunting W4

Single Sightings 1976-1987

The following species have been seen only once on, or flying over, Nose Hill during the period 1976 to 1987. About half of these species were seen in the section of Nose Hill west of Shaganappi Trail.

Many of these species are rare in Calgary except those marked ☆ which are seen annually in Calgary, but seldom on Nose Hill.

    Double-crested Cormorant
☆   Great Blue Heron
    Ferruginous Hawk
    Broad-winged Hawk
☆   Bald Eagle
    Gyrfalcon
☆   Mourning Dove
☆   Snowy Owl
    Black-billed Cuckoo
    Northern Saw-whet Owl
    Common Nighthawk
☆   Blue Jay
☆   Red-breasted Nuthatch
    Townsend's Solitaire
☆   Veery
    Warbling Vireo
    Tennessee Warbler
☆   Orange-crowned Warbler

Rosy Finch
Red Crossbill
☆ White-winged Crossbill
Harris' Sparrow
Swamp Sparrow

Mammals

Mammals which have been seen in the past, but which have probably been extirpated on Nose Hill (e.g. Bison), have been omitted from this list.

American Badger 1
Little Brown Bat 1
Coyote 2
Mule Deer 2
White-tailed Deer 1
Northern Plains Red Fox 1
Richardson Pocket Gopher 2
White-tailed Prairie Hare 2
Varying Hare 2
Lynx 1
Muskrat 1
Porcupine 2
Richardson Ground Squirrel 4
Meadow Vole 2
★ **Least Weasel** 1
Prairie Long-tailed Weasel 2
★ Common Striped Skunk 1
★ Jumping Mouse 1

Plate 1

Downtown Calgary from Nose Hill, with a glacial erratic, used by Buffalo as a rubbing-stone, in the foreground

Dave Elphinstone

Plate 2

Tipi Ring   *Dave Elphinstone*

South-facing Slopes & Ravines

Plate 3

Moss Phlox

see page 31

Gaillardia

see page 53

Plate 4

Star-flowered Solomon's Seal

see page 43

Plate 5

Wood's Rose

see page 47

Rose Hips — fruit of Wood's Rose

Plate 6

Early Blue Violet

see page 33

Sticky Purple Geranium

see page 54

Plate 7

Western Wood Lily *see page 56*

Golden Bean *see page 42*

Plate 8

Early Cinquefoil

see page 32

Western Canada Violet

see page 45

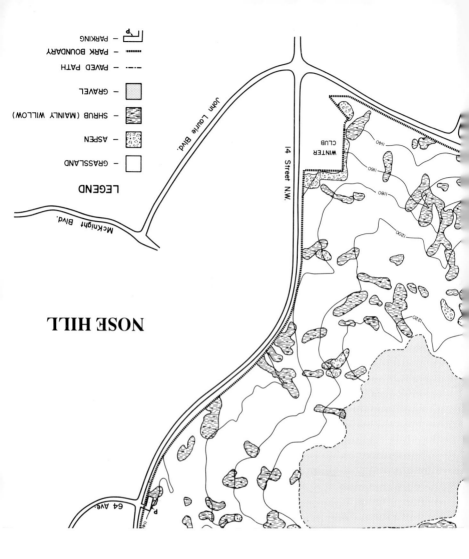

NOSE HILL

LEGEND

☐	—	GRASSLAND
▨	—	ASPEN
▦	—	SHRUB (MAINLY WILLOW)
▨	—	GRAVEL
—··—	—	PAVED PATH
········	—	PARK BOUNDARY
⌐P	—	PARKING

McKnight Blvd.

John Laurie Blvd.

14 Street N.W.

64 Ave.

WINTER CLUB

1140
1160
1180
1200
1220

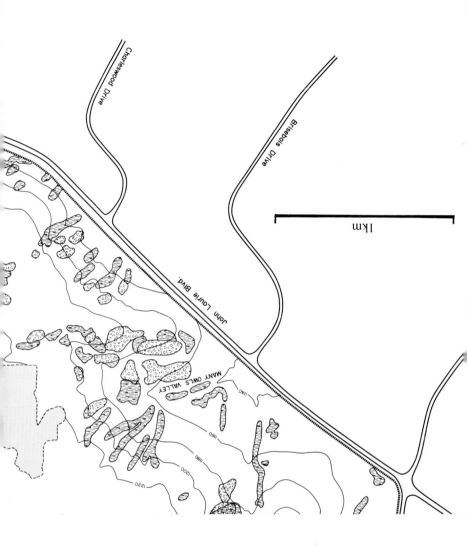

Charleswood Drive

Brisebois Drive

John Laurie Blvd.

MANY OWLS VALLEY

1140

1160

1180

1200

1220

1km